AFRICAN MUSIC:

A People's Art

FRANCIS BEBEY

FRANCIS BEBEY

AFRICAN MUSIC

A People's Art

Translated by Josephine Bennett

LAWRENCE HILL & COMPANY

New York · Westport

This book was produced for the publisher by Ray Freiman & Company.

Contents

Introduction

THE INTENTION of this book is to introduce the reader to the world of traditional African music. It is a world which until now has attracted scant public attention, partly because of its apparently highly-specialized nature, but also because it has previously been described in terms that have tended to imprison it inside the covers of scholarly treatises instead of making it accessible to all men. And yet, African sculpture and painting are at last beginning to move beyond conference halls frequented by Africanists to attract an ever-growing and increasingly enthusiastic public. Why then should music—an unrivaled black African art—be content with a mere handful of followers drawn from the ranks of those in search of exotic adventures or unusual rhythms and timbres?

African music is fundamentally a collective art. It is a communal property whose spiritual qualities are shared and experienced by all; in short, it is an art form that can and must communicate with people of all races and cultures and that should enjoy the ultimate fate of all the great currents of human thought—to make its mark on the present and the future, while bringing a new breath of life to all mankind. In order to do so, it must first be made accessible to all men everywhere; it must be explained to them and allowed to take root, germinate and flower in their cultural understanding. We are expounding on a process, not of popularization, but of dissemination, an investment programme with high hopes and expectations.

Our motive in undertaking this initiation into traditional African music is not merely that of a connoisseur bent on sharing the rare fruit of a genuine passion; rather, we are convinced of the need for other people to explore this unknown and exciting world. This is a world where we can learn more about mankind, a world pulsating with spiritual forces that unashamedly lays bare its inner truth and reveals the threshold of human happiness. The tropical forest is not populated by miserable savages, for, as African music can show us, such creatures do not exist. Our aim in writing this book is to convince the reader of this fact.

Literally dozens of books could be written on the subject of music, but they would be of little use without illustrations to support their respective texts.

In works of this kind, illustrations usually take the form of musical transcriptions. We have ruled out this method which would be meaningless for the many readers who cannot read music. In any case, musicologists have not yet found an accurate and satisfactory method of notation for African music. Instead, we have chosen to refer the reader directly to the music itself, as it is recorded.

We have tried to limit our choice of records to a minimum in order to avoid overwhelming any reader who may feel drawn to acquire some of them. We sincerely hope that he will feel so drawn, not only in order that he may gain a wider understanding of our subject, but more importantly, so that he will have his own personal documentation and points of reference.

In addition, we have included a selective discography at the end of the book that will give a comprehensive idea of what commercial catalogues have to offer. Finally, there is a very small, basic discography containing those records we consider indispensable for a first contact under optimum conditons.

Most of the records mentioned can be obtained from specialized dealers in the United States or in the United Kingdom.[1] It seemed futile to include material that is hard to find, such as tape recordings or records that are either obsolete or not readily available, particularly as many such recordings are not of the highest technical quality. The high-fidelity quality of present-day commercial recording undeniably enhances appreciation of the music itself.

Before we plunge into the heart of our subject, we should like to thank a number of organizations and individuals whose efforts to preserve and diffuse traditional African music have, in recent years, been marked by the production of excellent records. Without these records this book could not have been furnished with suitable examples. In particular, we wish to thank the Musée de l'Homme in Paris and Mr. Gilbert Rouget; the O.R.T.F. (the French National Radio and Television Broadcasting Organization); OCORA Records, Paris and Messrs Charles Duvelle and Tolia Nikiprowetzky—this organization has the largest catalogue of traditional African music in the world; Unesco and those of its experts who produced the records in the Anthology of African Music—a series of ten albums of great interest; and Folkways Records in the United States. To all of them we offer our warmest encouragements for an even greater output of continuing high quality.

F.B.

A man and his music dedicated to the service of all men; a people and its music for the happiness of everyone.

Expression of Life

AUTHENTIC AFRICAN music—the traditional music of the black peoples of Africa—is little known abroad. The non-African listener generally finds the music strange, difficult, and unattractive; therefore, he concludes that it is not of interest. This is by no means the case. However, the study of African music demands time and patience. Familiarity with its environment certainly helps and the student is invariably rewarded by finding this music extremely attractive.

Over the past thirty years, films, photographs, and records have brought certain aspects of African music, its musicians, and its cultural context to the attention of Western audiences. Unfortunately, however, the aim of most film producers and record companies is commercial success and thus they have tended to emphasize the exotic and the unexpected at the expense of the real substance. By so doing, they have rendered a serious disservice to African cultures generally and to music in particular. The initial curiosity of a Western audience can be followed all too easily by contempt for a way of life that is so unlike their own and by an inability to appreciate the music that seem to them to be so much dissonance and noise.

Westerners today, however, are beginning to pay more attention to these African cultures. In Europe, America, and Africa itself there have been numerous conferences over the past twenty years devoted to the cultural life of the peoples of black Africa. Particular evidence of this growing interest was shown at the First World Festival of Negro Arts held in Dakar, Senegal in April of 1966. Although the cinema has barely begun to produce films of authentic African life, record companies are at last issuing excellent recordings of authentic African music and television is giving more attention to the artistic and cultural world of Africa. Undoubtedly, there are ways of getting to know this new world, even without the luxury of a visit.

But there are no short cuts. A real understanding of African cultures demands hours of attention, the will to look and listen carefully, to reject preconceived ideas, and to avoid hasty judgments. Then perhaps, the striking differences that trouble the non-African can be turned to good account; for

1

the effort to understand may lead to the creation of new art forms and may influence future artistic creation.

The Westerner who wishes to understand the authentic music of Africa must be willing to reject the notion that it is "primitive" music consisting merely of rhythmic noises. This simple act of rejection will "open his ears" and allow him to discover gradually that African music in many respects resembles his own. Slowly, he can begin to pinpoint those differences which, if comprehended correctly, may enrich universal culture. African music is not the reserve of the intellectual; it is universal enough to be enjoyed by music lovers anywhere.

What form do the resemblances between the music of these two cultures assume? First and foremost, both African and Western music are an invention of man, at least as far as creation is concerned. Secondly, we find in both the same notions of instrumental or vocal music, low or high pitch, long or short, sustained or staccato notes. In both cases, music plays a similar role in life, as lullabies, battle songs, religious music, and so on. It is important in education; it is common knowledge that songs make memorizing easier and can be used to instill in people important rules of conduct or hygiene. Lastly, the musical instruments themselves provide perhaps the most important similarity between African and Western music. Generally speaking, the same categories of instruments are found in black Africa as in the West, namely stringed instruments, wind instruments, and percussion.

Despite these similarities, there are many reasons why Westerners find African music so bewildering. Broadly speaking, most Europeans would define music as "the art of combining sounds in a manner pleasing to the ear." While it is true that this conception has been questioned in recent years—most "pop" music and a great deal of so-called "serious" contemporary music could hardly be described as soothing to the ear—there is still a lingering notion that noise and music are incompatible.

Then again, many Westerners think of music as an expression of emotions. Actually, music is too abstract to be capable of rendering truly lifelike descriptions but Westerners are trained to seek certain signs. For instance, the major key is supposed to convey joy and the minor key sorrow, but there is no logical basis for this contention and the reverse could just as easily be true. In the fifteenth and sixteenth centuries the very popular minor mode was not necessarily used to indicate sorrow. In other words, Western music implies the existence of certain preconceived ideas and, while this is in no way intended as a criticism of Western music, it is evident that this hermetic approach does not facilitate the understanding of a music based on totally different premises.

Another factor which must not be overlooked is that in the West music is considered as a pure art form. Listening to music is a pleasure to be enjoyed for its own sake. People go to concerts or buy records simply to enjoy music. Those artists who combine music with another art, such as choreography, are all too rare. Music is used as an accompaniment to films or plays, rather than forming

Drums begin to throb and the dancers leap into action in the hastily formed circle of men and women—not forgetting the children.

an integral part of them. Even in opera, that true marriage of theatre and music, the latter can be divorced from the rest and enjoyed for its own sake. Music is an autonomous and independent art. It is barely an exaggeration to say that those newspapers that have separate columns devoted to ''The Arts'' and ''Music'' virtually imply that music is not an art at all!

For all these reasons and many others, Westerners are frequently at a loss to understand the music of black Africa: the concepts of Africans are so totally different. African musicians do not seek to combine sounds in a manner pleasing to the ear. Their aim is simply to express life in all of its aspects through the medium of sound. But, whereas Western music is rather an inadequate form of expression, the same can by no means be said of African music. The African musician does not merely attempt to imitate nature by means of musical instruments; he reverses the procedure by taking natural sounds and incorporating them into his music. To the uninitiated this may result in cacophony, but in fact each sound has a particular meaning, as those who have had firsthand experience of African life can testify. If it is to be meaning-

The average African child reveals a natural aptitude for music at a very early age.

ful African music must be studied within the context of traditional African life.

A French ethno-musicologist, Mr. Herbert Pepper, who spent eleven years among the forest-dwellers of the Congo and Gabon, has written:

"I had the impression that I learnt more about my art in the African school than in the Western school. The latter certainly taught me to appreciate the quality of the finished article, but it sometimes seemed so far removed from the everyday world that I began to wonder if it bore any relationship to it. The African school, on the other hand, has taught me that what matters is not the quality of the music itself, but its ability to render emotions and desires as naturally as possible."[1]

Children sometimes borrow the adults' drums to accompany their songs and dances.

This "African school" which Mr. Pepper discovered in adult life is the birthright of every African child. It is a school in the broadest sense, not merely a musical education, but a comprehensive preparation for that strange adventure upon which he is about to embark—life.

A lullaby, for instance, has a dual purpose—to comfort a baby and also to teach him why he should not cry:

> *Ye ye ya ye–Do not cry*
> *Think of our friends who are childless*
> *Hush, do not cry*
> *Think of those who have no children*
> *Think of my married brother*
> *Who has no children yet*
> *And then look at me*
> *I have a mother too*
> *But I don't cry*
> *Think of our friends who are childless*
> *Think of my brother*
> *Who married a Bacanda girl*
> *What an idea, to marry a Bacanda*
> *And they are still without children*
> *Don't cry, my darling*
> *Think of your unhappy father . . .*

This simple lullaby, like almost all African music, conveys a number of ideas simultaneously. Outwardly, it is intended to soothe the baby and lull him to sleep, but at the same time, it expresses his mother's gratitude toward Nature—or God—for having given her a child, a privilege denied to so many other women.

At this early stage in life, it is evident that the child is merely a listener, but as he begins to grow up, he very soon takes an active role in music. The average African child reveals a natural aptitude for music at a very early age. He is already making his own musical instruments at three or four; an empty tin becomes a rattle, an old window-frame and a piece of animal hide make a drum (which musicologists call a "frame-drum"). Whether or not he has the makings of a musician, his talents as a singer soon become apparent; music is an indispensable element in children's games. Youngsters of four or five love to imitate the songs and dances of their elders and, even at this age, their priorities are quickly established; any child who is more interested in eating than singing is a subject of derision. It is also clear that talent has nothing to do with age, for the rhythms that these tiny tots hammer out on their makeshift instruments are a portent of their capabilities in later life.

These five-year-olds have just made their first musical instrument from a length of raffia stalk; it is a zither which takes three young musicians to play.

Thus, music is clearly an integral part of the life of every African individual from the moment of his birth. The musical games played by children are never gratuitous; they are a form of musical training which prepares them to participate in all areas of adult activity—fishing, hunting, farming, grinding maize, attending weddings, funerals, dances, and by necessity, even fleeing from wild animals. This explains why every conceivable sound has its place in traditional African music, whether in its natural form as it is produced by the object or animal in question, or reproduced by an instrument that imitates them as faithfully as possible.

It was no doubt this extremely concrete aspect of African music that prompted Leopold Sédar Senghor to remark that recent Western experiments with "musique concrète" are but a belated attempt to catch up with a musical form that has been practiced in Africa for many hundreds of years. A particularly striking example of this is the bull-roarer. The music (perhaps noise would be a more appropriate term) of this elementary little instrument has a deep significance totally belied by the simplicity of its appearance.

The bull-roarer consists of a rectangular piece of bamboo or wood (occasionally metal) about a foot long with a piece of string attached to one end. The other end of the string is held in the hand and the instrument is swung in a circle, so that it revolves vertically on its own axis. The faster it spins, the louder is the noise that is produced. To a Westerner, it may sound rather like a car engine starting up, but to West African children, it represents the roaring of a panther.

The panther is greatly feared and the adults are generally not pleased to be reminded of it by the children who are playing with their bull-roarers and adults sometimes tell them to "stop calling the panther like that." The appearance of a panther in an equatorial village is the signal for a general stampede, which is particularly disagreeable for the menfolk who temporarily cease to be all-powerful and thus lose their traditional superiority over the women and children. In certain West African tribes, such as the *Dogon* of Mali, the sound of the bull-roarer signals the end of the funeral rite that terminates a period of mourning. On such occasions, the masks make their appearance. The ceremony begins at nightfall when an initiate rotates the bull-roarer to warn the women and children that they must disappear, for they are not permitted to see the masks. The musician continues to play the bull-roarer all night, leading the procession of masks around the deserted village. The *Dogon* believe the bull-roarer to be the voice of their ancestor, the first man who encountered death; it also symbolizes the revelation of speech to mankind.

This curious little instrument provides a great deal of invaluable information about the importance of the symbol in African life. It is also interesting to note that in different contexts and regions the bull-roarer invariably symbolizes power of one kind or another: the power of the males, jealously protected against the panther; the power of the ancestor whose death has been transmitted down from generation to generation; the power of speech whose revelation has given man supremacy over all the other creatures on earth. Perhaps the most

Music is an indispensable element in children's games.

Expression of Life

fascinating aspect of this ritual is the attitude of the male; when the panther— the real panther—roars, everyone hides, leaving the panther to prowl outside the huts in solitary splendour. When the bull-roarer is heard, on the other hand, the women and children disappear and it is only then that the men who wear the masks begin their nocturnal parade through the village. In other words, the male seizes this opportunity to display the power which, in other cir- cumstances, the panther could dispute. Here we have another symbol.

But although musical games have an extremely important educational function, they present only a fraction of adult life; a life that begins in earnest when the adolescent is admitted into adult society at the time of his initiation. Music plays a paramount role in this initiation; it is as vital to the ceremonies as are the children themselves. And having been a constant factor throughout the child's life, there is no logical reason why music should recede into the background at the time of initiation. It is not merely used as an accompaniment to the ceremonies, but has its own well-defined role to play. A particularly striking example of this role is to be found among the *Adiukru* of the Ivory Coast. During the graduation ceremonies from one age-class to another, tom- toms assume the attributes of real human beings; they speak to the young men

These youngsters love to imitate the songs and dances of their elders.

Every conceivable sound has its place in traditional African music. Here, the steady pounding of the pestles in the mortar provides the rhythmic accompaniment to the songs of the women as they grind.

Expression of Life

who answer them. Then, the young people talk to the tom-toms who "listen" and reply.[2] A real conversation takes place between the musical instruments and the men who made them, a dialogue between music and its creator—man. This intimate union between man and art is rare outside of Africa. It amounts to a total communion that is shared by the whole community. It may help to explain why some languages in black Africa have no precise noun to define music. The *Duala* of Cameroon have adopted the word *musiki* (pronounced *moossiki*) from the French *musique*. They have their own words to define specific forms, such as *elongi* (song) or *ngoso* (chant), but these can by no means be considered generic terms. The art of music is so inherent in man that it is superfluous to have a particular name for it.

The initiation cermony of the *Adiukru* (Ivory Coast) referred to above is known as *lohu*. Its purpose is to admit a number of adolescents into adult society. During a certain period of time before the ceremony, the boys have to wear women's clothing and allow their hair to grow long. At the end of the *lohu* their hair is cut and their normal clothing restored. As soon as they are again

As they dance, it is the bells round the dancers' ankles that now provide a rhythmic accompaniment to the music.

A sure sign of dignity: This drum, supported by four men, is regarded as a very important person.

Expression of Life

dressed as men they careen wildly around the village and then form an orderly procession to take part in the conversation with the drums. The ceremony concludes with singing and dancing.

Because the drum is, in certain circumstances, equated with a man (and a rather exceptional man, at that, whose powerful voice is capable of sending messages far and wide), women must consequently treat it with the same respect that they show towards their menfolk. No woman would dream of beating her husband in public (even though she may occasionally do so in private!), nor may she beat the drum in the village square. In some African societies, women are not even permitted to touch a drum under any circumstance. In other societies, particularly those that have adopted the Islamic faith, certain types of drums may be played by women, for example, the water-drum or the *bendere* calabash drum found in Upper Volta. However, the evolution of

African music, which is nearly always coupled with some other art form, expresses the feelings and life of the entire community. The sound of feet pounding the ground becomes the rhythm of the music whose notes are in turn transformed into dance steps.

Wielded by a man in the service of music, these enormous wicker rattles reproduce the rhythm of the ocean waves.

the Christian Church in black Africa during the last twenty years and the "africanization" of the Catholic mass and Protestant choir have given rise to sights that some Africans find profoundly shocking; for example, women playing tom-toms or xylophones in church. The introduction into church services of instruments that had for generations been considered unworthy of such holy places has, not surprisingly, met with some disapproval. This is just one aspect of the African revolution that began toward the end of the Second World War and culminated spectacularly in the end of colonial rule. This socio-philosophical aspect of the black world, which is no less important than the political and economic aspects, provides the context in which African music must be considered. Moreover, any attempt to follow the meaning and evolution of African music will, surprising as it may seem, shed a great deal of light on the evolution of African society in general and will help to clarify the apparent ambiguity of that society's own individual brand of logic.

In fact, African music which is an "impure" art form in that it is nearly always coupled with some other art, such as poetry or dance, is without doubt one of the most revealing forms of expression of the black soul. The effort to understand it may be hard, but the reward will be all the greater. Under a rather forbidding exterior of unmelodious noise, peculiar notes and scales, rudimentary instruments, and strange tonalities, lies the whole of African life and the expression of all of its many human qualities.

The African Musician

HAVING ESTABLISHED two basic facts—that music is an integral part of African life from the cradle to the grave and that African music covers the widest possible range of expression, including spoken language and all manner of natural sounds—it may seem logical to conclude that everyone in black Africa must, by definition, be a musician. This is not necessarily the case in practice. It is true that most Africans do have a natural sense of rhythm which is one of the most characteristic features of African music. This instinct for rhythm not only produces a large number of talented percussionists, but also enables many Africans to master the techniques of more complicated melodic instruments. Nevertheless, it would be a mistake to assume that all Africans are necessarily musicians in the full sense of the word. Africans themselves are fully conscious of this fact.

In numerous African societies, the right to play certain instruments or to participate in traditional ceremonies is not open to all. Strict rules govern the choice of instruments to be used on specific occasions and the musicians who are permitted to play them. In Rwanda, for example, the privilege of playing the six royal drums, which were the royal emblems of the *Mwami* (the king of the *Tutsi* people), was reserved for one particular musician.[1] In other communities, only young people of the most outstanding ability may entertain the hope of being called to fill the place vacated by the death of one of the "official" drummers. Such an event is marked by an important ceremony in which the late musician officially relegates his position to his successor. The musician's corpse is seated before the drum that he used to play in his lifetime and the drum-stick is placed in his right hand. An elder of the tribe, or the orchestra leader, moves the dead man's hand so that the stick touches the drum-head. Then, the new recruit takes the drum-stick and strikes the drum in exactly the same spot. He is then considered to be officially invested and may take his place in the community's orchestra.

There are, however, other African societies in which music is not the privilege of a caste of specialists, but is a dynamic and driving force that animates the life of the entire community. This communal music may be quite elaborate in form, as is the case of the Pygmies who inhabit the equatorial forest. They live by hunting, gathering wild fruits, and bartering with villages on the edge of the forest; all their daily occupations are accompanied by music. Men and women, young and old alike, contribute their share to the collective enjoyment by singing, clapping, stamping, and other rhythmic actions. All Pygmies are musicians, otherwise they would be incapable of participating fully in the nomadic life of this race of hunters. Pygmy music is usually very sophisticated in rhythm and form, as well as in its ritual structure. Pygmies rarely sing in unison; the songs they perform to celebrate a successful hunting expedition are polyphonic in form with a fairly simple rhythmic pattern provided by handclapping and sticks struck one against another. Although their

A fine hunter and an excellent musician—a true Pygmy

The history of a town such as Timbuctoo owes just as much to the memory of these Tuareg musicians as it does to the written word.

songs are constructed within a very strict framework, the performers are left with great freedom to improvise. In this type of community where everyone is a musician, the artist usually has no particular place in society to single him out from the rest.

In other societies musicians form a semiprofessional group. They earn their livelihood from their music for only part of the year and they rely on some other activity for the remainder of the time. There are *Bambara* farmers in Upper Volta who leave their fields every year during the dry season in order to travel hundreds of miles with their musical instruments. They go from village to village, enlivening local festivities with their playing and singing. They usually expect those who benefit from their visit to pay for the pleasure that they provide.

Music is by no means a profitable occupation for everyone in these communities. What is it, then, which attracts certain people toward music? Here is one answer which a semiprofessional harp-lute player from the Ivory Coast gave to Mr. Hugo Zemp:

". . . I was working at my loom one day, as usual, when suddenly I saw two dwarf-genii, who said to me, 'Get up! Go home and hang yourself.' None of the other weavers could see them. I left the loom and went home. I found a length of rope, attached it to a roof-beam and hanged myself. Some of the villagers had followed me home, so they cut the rope and then went to consult a soothsayer. He told them that in the past some of my relatives had been harp-lute players and unless I continued the tradition I was doomed to die. There had been no harp-lute player in our village since my father's brother died. My relatives found the instrument, which had not been touched since my uncle's death, and sacrificed a chicken. Then I set about learning to play the harp-lute. As soon as it became known that I had been ordered to play the harp-lute the people of all the neighbouring villages in the district began inviting me to play for them and I received many presents. Sometimes I was away travelling for weeks at a stretch. But during the farming season I always stayed at home to work on my plantation."[2]

Because of a dream—or a vision—a man who had never touched a musical instrument before in his life became the best harp-lute player in his region. How did he intend to pass on his art? Would he teach his own children to play or did he look upon it as a personal gift? Here is his own reply: "I'm not dead yet, so I can't teach anyone else to play the instrument. When I die the dwarf-genii will choose my successor. It could even be someone who isn't a member of my family."

We have not quoted this *Baule* musician's actual words, which may appear rather naive, with the intention of amusing the reader, but rather, in order to illustrate the mystical, almost magical relationship that can exist between a man and his music. The fact that his vocation was prompted by some kind of supernatural revelation shows how closely magic and music are related

Magic and music—their secret is one and the same.

in African society. Perhaps the similarity of the two words in English is not merely coincidental.

In this particular case, the element of magic went a stage further. The musician also relates that when the dwarf-genii ordered him to play the harp-lute, he was also given the secret of a cure for leprosy which he apparently used with great success. The use of the harp in healing leprosy is by no means exceptional; this instrument is invariably associated with the powers of healing that are granted by spirits. Nor is the experience of this musician from the Ivory Coast in any way out of the ordinary; all *Baule* harp players are known to communicate with the spirit world. This characteristic is echoed in many other African tribes. Most harp-lute players are also soothsayers or healers.

This story also demonstrates that people sometimes learn to play an instrument because they have been more or less forced to do so. Music is a communal undertaking and people tend to become musicians not so much from personal vocation as from a need to fulfill a social obligation. In this instance, the community needed a new harp-lute player. The choice of who he was to be was left to the dwarf-genii.

Semiprofessional musicians are not always, like the one we have mentioned above, isolated individuals. Very often they belong to one particular trade or caste, such as the *Senufo* orchestras that are composed of groups of blacksmiths, farmers, and other tribesmen.

Finally, we come to those African societies that have professional musicians. Such musicians live solely by their art and belong to particular families or castes. Their music is much more esoteric and is transmitted from one generation to another. These families or castes may be recognized by their characteristic surnames. *Keita, Mamadi, Diubate* or *Dibate, Kuyate,* and *Sory* are all names usually associated with *griots,* although it is not unusual now to come across people with these names who have received a European education and who have branched out into a profession quite different from that of their ancestors.

Griot is the term used throughout West Africa to designate a professional musician. What exactly is a *griot*? It may be easier to begin by saying what a *griot* is not. Contrary to popular belief, a *griot* is not merely an African witch doctor or sorcerer, although some *griots* do dabble in witchcraft. They usually specialize in the art of invoking supernatural beings of all kinds and sing their praises in order to ensure their pardon, protection or goodwill. However, the role of the *griot* in West African society extends far beyond the realm of magic. The fact that music is at the heart of all the *griot'*s activities is yet further proof of the vital part he plays in African life.

Few European travelers who have actually met a *griot* have grasped the meaning of the role that he plays in society and they tend to make hasty and erroneous judgments. The French novelist, Pierre Loti, is no exception and concludes his description of *griots* in *Roman d'un Spahi* with these words: "Griots are the most philosophical and the laziest people in the world. They

When the griot sings, even the sun at its zenith stops to listen.

The African Musician

lead a nomadic life and never worry about tomorrow.'' This rather uncharitable view does at least have the merit of placing the *griot* in his true perspective in time; he is more concerned with the past than with the future. By the past, we mean not only the history of his people—its kings and ancestors, and the genealogy of its great men—but also, the wisdom of its philosophers, its corporate ethics and generosity of spirit, its thought-provoking riddles, and the ancestral proverbs that serve as a reminder that everything on earth is destined to pass, just as time itself passes.

The West African *griot* is a troubadour, the counterpart of the medieval European minstrel. Some *griots* are attached to the courts of noblemen, others are independent and go from house to house, or from village to village, peddling stories and adding new ones to their collection. The *griot* knows everything that is going on and he can recall events that are no longer within living memory. He is a living archive of his people's traditions. But he is above all a musician, without whom no celebration or ritual would be complete. His repertoire is extremely wide and ranges from set pieces for special occasions such as weddings and christenings to songs in praise of individual customers that are composed to order. *Griots* who belong to the household of a nobleman are appointed to extol the glories and virtues of their master. Independent *griots* sing the praises of anyone who can afford to pay them and it would be the height of folly to haggle over the price. They are quick to flatter those who reward them well, but a discontented *griot* would not hesitate to slander and curse a less generous client and to brand him with the reputation of being a miser.

The virtuoso talents of the *griot* command universal admiration. This virtuosity is the culmination of long years of study and hard work under the tuition of a teacher who is often a father or uncle. The profession is by no means a male prerogative. There are many women *griots* whose talents as singers and musicians are equally remarkable.

Although the talents of these extraordinary musicians are much admired, it must be admitted that they rarely enjoy personal esteem. People fear them because they know too many secrets. They are often treated with contempt, and in fact, belong to one of the lowest castes in the social hierarchy along with the shoemakers, weavers, and blacksmiths. This attitude that prevails toward them is reflected in the legend that recounts how the ancestor of the *griots* came into being.

It tells of two brothers travelling through the forest. They were striding along bravely in the heat of the sun when the younger one was suddenly seized by violent pangs of hunger and said to his brother, ''You'd better carry on and finish the journey alone. I can't go a step further. I'm dying of hunger.'' The elder brother pretended to agree and went on alone. But, as soon as he was hidden from sight behind a large clump of bushes, he stopped, drew out his knife, and cut a piece of flesh from his own thigh. He prepared the meat carefully and took it back to his brother who ate ravenously. He soon regained his strength and they set off again. After a little while, however, the younger

Contrary to popular belief, a griot is not a kind of African witchdoctor, but primarily an extraordinarily gifted musician.

one noticed that his brother was covered with bloodstains. He asked him what had happened, but he received no reply. Finally, when they had reached the next village, his elder brother confessed what he had done to help him, whereupon the younger brother made the following vow: ''In order to save me from death, you did not hesitate to give me the flesh of your own thigh. Henceforth, I shall be called *Dieli,* your servant, and all my descendants will serve your descendants.'' This is how *Dieli,* the ancestor of the *griots,* is said to have originated and the name is still used today by the *Fali* of Guinea and the *Bambara* of Mali to designate *griots.*

This legend explains allegorically why *griots* have come to occupy such a lowly rank in society. There is no escape from the rank even after death. In some parts of West Africa, *griots* were not allowed the right to a proper burial. People believed that if a *griot's* body was buried in the normal manner, it would render the earth perpetually barren. When a *griot* died his body was placed inside the hollow trunk of a gigantic baobab tree. A tree-cemetery of this kind was discovered some years ago in Dakar (Senegal). The huge trunk contained a vast quantity of bones.[3]

This mixture of admiration and scorn, which is the lot of a class of men whose very existence depends upon what they find to say about other people, reminds us of the words of Aesop, the ancient Greek fabulist. When asked why he considered the tongue to be both the best and worst of things, he replied, "Because it can not only be used to praise the gods but is also an organ of blasphemy."

"Whether they are looked upon as the upholders of tradition or the inventors of new melodies, poems and rhythms, their existence," says André Jolivet, "has one supreme merit: it is a striking example of the importance of music and the musician. It is not altogether displeasing that this truth should be brought home to us by people who may still be young politically speaking, but whose roots are firmly established in the primordial forces of nature, from which they draw the essence of their material and spiritual life."[4]

The disrespect and scorn shown to the *griot* by his own community has the rather dubious advantage of illustrating some of the general problems indigenous to the African artist in society. Recent conferences on African art and culture have reproached Africans, sometimes in rather harsh terms, for not always recognizing the true place of the artist in society; that is to say, in a new African society that has evolved considerably from traditional African communities. Governments and cultural centres are being urged to study the problem of the African artist in hopes of according him his rightful place—a place of honour, needless to say. However, it must never be forgotten that despite this evolution in African society, we are still dealing with peoples of tradition and two important facts usually seem to be overlooked. In the first place, people tend to forget that in African communities where art is a living and popular birthright, the artist, far from being scorned, usually occupies an enviable position in society. For instance, the medicine man or healer encourages the entire community to participate in the dances that he employs as part of his therapy and no one would ever dream of relegating him to an inferior position. The role of those artists who are essential to initiation ceremonies— ceremonies that are a combination of philosophy, mythology, technique, and art—leaves no doubt as to their importance in society. The other fact that should not be forgotten is that the art of the *griot* is essentially contemplative (hence static), individualistic, and preeminently self-interested. It is not orientated toward the future, but firmly entrenched in the past. It is not a collective art form; this is a distinct disadvantage in societies where art is regarded as a communal undertaking. When the *griot* speaks or sings, he expects immediate

The drum is not the only instrument of the griots, nor for that matter is it the sum total of African music.

attention and he is ready with an insult if such attention is not forthcoming. Most *griots* are self-seeking and would not deign to perform unless they were sure of their reward, either in money or in kind. If we take all these facts into account it is clear that the problem of the *griot* is not, as it may at first seem, common to all African artists. Rather, the *griot* is a special case that must be treated separately.

Leaving these arguments aside, it cannot be denied that *griots* are extraordinary musicians with outstanding talent who play an extremely important role in their respective societies. Their knowledge of the customs of the people and courtly life in all countries where they exercise their art gives them definite advantages; for the whole life of the people, its monarch, and ministers, is preserved intact in the infallible memory of the *griots*.

The equivalent of the *griot* in equatorial Africa is the player of the *mvet* or harp-zither. He may not be as well-known outside of Africa as the *griot,* but he is no less interesting or less famous within his own society. There, he combines the multiple functions of musician, dancer, story-teller, and storehouse of oral tradition. He is, in some ways, more fortunate than the *griot* for the admiration that he enjoys is not tinged with scorn. This is probably due to the fact that the *mvet* player's repertoire does not normally include the improvised songs that are composed to order in praise of the rich. The repertoire of the *Fang mvet* players of south Cameroon and Gabon, for instance, consists mainly of stories, epic legends, heroic deeds, and marvels—a favourite topic being the struggle for power between the mortals and immortals. "On earth, Ovang-Obam-O-Ndong, aided by Ondo Zogo (whose weapon is a withered human arm) is recruiting an army of volunteers in an attempt to capture immortality from the kingdom of Engong, where it is closely guarded by the chieftain, Akoma Mba.

Music as a sales technique: This vendor of talismans and amulets attracts his clients' attention by singing the praises of his wares.

Many trials await him when he enters this kingdom, but he will overcome them bravely with the help of his army. But, at the end of the poem (which lasts a whole night) he will once again fail in his undertaking.''[5]

The *mvet* is a kind of harp-zither. The strings are stretched along a raffia-palm stalk and raised over a bridge situated halfway along the stalk. The sound is amplified by a sound-box consisting of one or more gourds. The musician himself is usually bare to the waist and beside a raffia skirt, he is adorned with necklaces, bracelets, and a large quantity of feathers. He is an amusing sight for foreign eyes, perhaps, but as soon as he makes his appearance in the village square he is surrounded by an excited crowd. He has only to sketch a dance movement and all the jingling bells and beads he wears round his ankles and wrists invite the onlookers to gather around and dance with him. He has only to hum the first few notes of the verse of a song and, as though by magic, the crowd seems to find the corresponding chorus. After these preliminaries, the eagerly awaited story begins in earnest and the audience settles down for the night; the end of the tale will come only with the dawn.

> Then they came to the Tribe-of-Visions
> Commanded by Ondo-Minko-M-Obiang
> r . . . r . . . r . . . r . . . (sound of a marching army)
> And then - just imagine!
> Ondo-Minko-M-Obiang the crocodile-man
> Began shouting at the top of his voice:
> 'The idiots! Where on earth are they going?
> Look at the way they march!
> Hey! Stop!'
> (Then, leaping forward): Kilit! Vivm! Hi! (onomatopoeia)
> He barred the road to the army
> And challenged Ondo-Zogo:
> 'What's happening? Where are you going?'
> And Ondo-Zogo of the Tribe-of-the-Strong-Hands
> Replied:
> 'We are going to the land of Engong-Nzok
> To see Mobege, the brother of Mba, from the village
> Of Fatu-Fe-Meneno.'
> (Ondo-Minko-M-Obiang): 'Who is your chief?'
> (Ondo-Zogo): 'Ovang-Obam-O-Ndong
> Of the Tribe-of-the-Fog.'
> And do you know what happened next?
> This crocodile-man Ondo-Minko-M-Obiang
> Ordered:
> 'You shall not pass!'
> And striking his chest with a resounding blow
> He drew from his mouth a great crocodile stone,
> Which he threw with all his might

In Ondo-Zogo's face, where it broke.
Ondo-Zogo of the Tribe-of-the-Strong-Hands
Staggered like someone about to fall
But, listen carefully, in spite of that he straightened up,
Brandished the withered arm he carried as a weapon . . .
And struck Ondo-Minko-M-Obiang
A violent blow on the mouth: Tos! (onomatopoeia)
So hard that all his teeth fell out: Folot - Folot (onomatopoeia)
And then - would you believe it? - Ondo-Minko-M-Obiang just stood there
With his teeth in his hand
Watching the column pass by. Yi, yi, yi, yi (laughter).

The laughter that interrupts the story at this point corresponds to the falling of the curtain at the end of an act. The audience, which has been listening intently up to this point, relaxes for a few moments while the *mvet* player asks, "What can your ears hear?" and the crowd shouts back, "They can hear the *mvet*." So the *mvet* strikes up, sometimes in solo and sometime to accompany a song in which the entire audience participates. After this interval comes the next episode in the long story of Ovang-Obam-O-Ndong among the immortals.

This repertoire, a mixture of music and epic poetry, is extremely ancient and has remained constant in form and content for many generations. This would seem to justify the words of Mr. André Schaeffner of the Musée de l'Homme in Paris who writes, "In the universal history of music the African Negro, like the Arab, is not really a creative musician but a natural musician, in the fundamental sense of the word."[6] However, we must point out that a *griot* who recites the family tree of a king or a harp-zither player who retraces the legendary steps of the heroes who set out to conquer immortality represents only one aspect of the African musician. And even within this unchanging framework of content and form, there is always plenty of scope for improvisation and ornamentation so that individual musicians can reveal their own particular talents and aptitudes. Thus, no two performances of any one piece will be exactly alike. Admittedly, Mr. Schaeffner goes on to add that the African musician is "amazingly gifted, sensitive to the slightest influences and capable of assimilating them without losing his own identity." What greater proof could there be that the African musician has a personality of his own, which is without any shadow of doubt an attribute of any creative artist? Mr. Schaeffner also points out that the black man is both "sensitive and distorting"; but in art, distortion can result in the creation of new forms. In fact, this so-called "natural" musician makes a true contribution to the evolution of his art precisely because he enjoys distorting what he borrows from nature or from other people. In other words, his "naturalism" is by no means a foregone conclusion and it should certainly not be equated with "primitiveness" merely because many of the instruments used in black Africa are archaic. The African

The mvet *harp-zither of the Fang story-teller is the African counterpart of the Greek bard's lyre.*

"Then they came to the Tribe-of-Visions Commanded by Ondo-Minko-M-Obiang . . ."

is fully conscious of his art and capable of approaching it imaginatively. He is certainly "open" to influences and does tend to "simplify", but it is not true to say that "although he proves to be open, he tends to withdraw into a dark, naïve universe which is his and his alone." This statement is inaccurate in regard to several points. This "universe" is not exclusive to the musician, for music is a collective art and the musician's basic role is to guide and coordinate. Second-ly, it is not at all a "naïve universe"; the musician knows the precise sig-nificance of his music and its role in society. His apparent naïvety is deceptive and can only mislead those whose acquaintance with him does not penetrate deeply enough. In this particular context of mysticism and faith, the term "naïvety" makes absolutely no sense. Faith is the universal armour which protects all avant-garde creative artists from the slings and arrows of criticism.

Finally, the universe of the African musician is anything but "dark". It glows with the radiance of life itself. The funeral music of the *Dogon* of Mali or the *Fali* of Cameroon demonstrates their refusal to accept death. Rather, they substitute the notion of metamorphosis into a bird or snake for that of death. They have a wealth of satirical songs that mock the idea of death "which would like us to believe that when it arrives we stop living." It is hardly likely that anyone with such a deep faith in life—especially an artist—would withdraw into a "dark" universe.

No, the black musician is not naïve, but what sometimes puzzles the non-African is the simplicity with which a black musician approaches his art. He does not reserve his extraordinary talents for his immediate circle, but shares them with anyone who is willing to listen. He rarely considers himself superior to others. Even the greatest musicians whose fame has spread throughout their country, thanks to the radio, rarely behave like celebrities. Many Europeans are amazed to see first-rate African musicians agreeing to record for the radio without any payment. In other climes, a good musician automatically assumes he will be paid the fees he deserves. If we leave aside the *griots*, it is rare to come across anyone in traditional African society who thinks of his music as his sole means of livelihood. More than one recording company has exploited the generosity of the African musician. In the 1950s, many 78 r.p.m. records of traditional and more modern African music were made under such circumstances with the artists sometimes being rewarded with nothing more than a bottle of locally brewed beer.

This, then, is the African musician—an artist who dedicates himself to the service of the community at large. Times change, but in Africa today this is true as never before. The African continent is developing rapidly and the attractions of urban life have set in motion an ever-increasing rural exodus. Each year, hundreds of young people leave their traditional environment where music has such a special meaning and are engulfed in towns where only a handful of individuals attempt to keep alive some of the customs of village life. The process of development cannot be halted and it will not spare traditional music or its exponents. Traditional musicians must, therefore, prepare to defend themselves against the inroads of modern times and try to ensure that their music will evolve in a way that will safeguard its authenticity.

One of greatest dangers facing the traditional African musician today is an inferiority complex engendered by the knowledge that most townspeople prefer the imported music dispensed, rather over-generously perhaps, by the radio and on records. In the past twenty years, these two mass media have opened the floodgates to a literal invasion of imported musical forms and they have already succeeded in making some Africans virtually forget the existence of the music of their traditional societies. In such circumstances the musician feels obliged either to abandon his so-called primitive art altogether or to attempt to bring it up-to-date. We once recorded a *Lobi* xylophone player who exemplifies the problem confronting the musician. This musician from the north of Ghana had arrived in Accra only two days before we met him and he soon encountered some people from his own tribe who invited him to listen to some European and American pop records. They were so full of enthusiasm for these talented foreign musicians that they managed to persuade him to abandon the "primitive" music he performed so brilliantly on his xylophone. Within two days, Kakarba had produced four new pieces, using borrowed jazz rhythms and a delicate ballad style which ill-suited his xylophone, particularly as the scale of the instrument bore precious little resemblance to those found in pop music. However, we agreed to record him, because we believed in all sincerity that these efforts to modernize his music deserved encouragement even though they were founded on an inexplicable feeling of guilt. After he had performed his new compositions, we begged him to play some of the authentic tunes of his village. He was rather reluctant at first, believing that after the masterly performance he had just given, his traditional music would come as an anticlimax. However, after an exhausting session, he finally had the chance to listen to everything he had recorded and he was the first to admit that the typically African themes were infinitely more beautiful and more expertly played than his attempts at modernization. Despite all the attractions of imported music and a conviction that his art must evolve, here was a musician intelligent enough to acknowledge the beauty of his traditional art.

The story of this particular musician illustrates another vital factor; in their own communities, musicians have no way of knowing what their own music sounds like and the tape recorder can be of enormous benefit to them. Our friend from northern Ghana had certainly never before in his life heard his own music as it sounded to an audience. To sit and to listen to it properly through a loudspeaker, as though he were listening to someone else, was nothing short of a revelation for him. The story has a happy ending because we managed to convince Kakarba of the validity of his village music which he decided not to abandon after all. One hopes that material difficulties will never force him to trade his traditional culture for the comforts of modern life.

Such difficulties are, indeed, another of the dangers which threaten traditional art as a whole, and music in particular; like most of his fellow-citizens, the African musician is feeling the effects of the revolution that is sweeping the entire continent and is raising expectations of higher standards of living which only a lucrative form of employment can satisfy. Music, as it is conceived in traditional society, is not a function which enables its exponents to meet the demands of modern life. Moreover, as we have already pointed out, the competition is enormous and under these conditions music as a profession offers very little opportunity. In some societies, music is not conceived as a profession at all, a fact which is even more limiting. As things exist today, then, traditional music is threatened with eventual extinction and will gradually disappear unless immediate steps are taken to assure the future of its most essential ingredient—the musician himself.

A master of ceremonies sometimes leads the dance in the manner of an orchestra conductor.

The African Musician

The West is at last becoming aware of the cultural value of African music and a number of people who live outside of Africa are making prodigious efforts to preserve this particular art form. Thanks to the activities of various recording companies, an increasing number of well-documented records are now available (many of which will be mentioned in more detail later in this book). Record libraries that store all types of folk music on tape are springing up in Europe and America. An excellent system of cataloguing makes it comparatively easy to locate any given item, from a *Fulani* flute solo to a *Malinke* lullaby. We should single out the efforts undertaken in France by OCORA Records who make and distribute excellent records of the traditional

The tape recorder can enable a musician to discover his own music when he hears it for the first time.

... to keep their ancestral musical treasures intact and hand them down in the traditional manner to the younger generations.

music of the peoples of black Africa and who have a record library that is a model of its kind. We shall come back to these impressive achievements at a later time but presently we feel compelled to state that in our opinion preservation is not enough. The recording, preservation, and diffusion of traditional African music must be accompanied by a parallel effort to preserve and emancipate the men who create this music—to provide them with a favourable

climate in which to progress so that they can gradually take their rightful palce in universal culture. Unless these things are accomplished, and accomplished quickly, African music will be unable to offer the world more than a fraction of its fresh and invigorating lifeblood.
d invigorating life-blood.

This does not imply that the traditional African musician should be sheltered from the infiltration of foreign influences. Such infiltration may, of course, represent a certain danger, but it can also be a source of artistic enrichment. We believe that a combination of different artistic and cultural values can, in some cases, have a beneficial effect, but only when the native artist is fully conscious of their respective merits. To avoid succumbing prematurely to foreign influences, it is vitally important for the artist to begin by acquiring a thorough knowledge of them. The African musician must begin by familiarizing himself with the music of his own social environment and that of other African societies. Only then should he embark on a detailed study of non-African music—European music in particular. After this period of apprenticeship, the musician will, if he so desires, be equipped to venture into the extremely delicate field that is known as the ''marriage of cultures.''

This is often a matter of intuition rather than a logical and scientific act of reasoning. If the assimilation has gone deep enough, a composer can no longer consciously weigh the proportion of European and African music he pours into his work in order to obtain satisfactory results; the assimilation will happen automatically.

However, we must be realistic and face the situation constructively. Africa today has innumerable problems to solve and music, despite its importance, is only one among many others. It may be years before the majority of traditional African musicians have the opportunity to reach that perfect assimilation of differing musical values that is so essential to the evolution of the music of the African continent. For the present, therefore, it may be wiser to concentrate on encouraging villagers to keep their ancestral musical treasures intact and to hand them down in the traditional manner to the younger generations. In this way, we hope that the time will come when a future generation of Africans will have both the knowledge and the opportunity to operate a synthesis of cultures.

Encouraging the African musician is the only way to ensure the survival of traditional music and enable it to make its full contribution to universal culture.

The Musical Instruments

BLACK AFRICA POSSESSES an infinite variety of musical instruments that is unrivaled except perhaps in Asia. Some of these instruments are made with consummate skill (*kora, balaphon,* drums, *sanzi, mvet*), while others—particularly certain types of xylophone—appear to have been casually thrown together, but they all have one thing in common; they are never mass-produced. The absence of machinery rules out industrial manufacture and the craft of instrument-making is a much more individual endeavor than it is among Western craftsmen. Instrument-making depends largely upon the natural materials available and their dimensions, rather than upon established norms that would almost automatically guarantee instruments to be of a standard quality. The size of a *Kora* a determined by the dimension of the calabash from which it is made. It follows that every musical instrument of its particular kind is unique; its general characteristics correspond to those others of its type, but it has its own individual beauty—its own qualities and defects.

Furthermore, professional craftsmen who specialize in instrument-making are extremely rare in Africa. Generally speaking, each musician makes his own instrument to suit his own particular tastes. He also "teaches" the instrument the language it will "speak," which is, of course, the musician's own mother tongue. Two *mvet* that are made by musicians from different tribes do not "speak" the same language. The Senegalese *Kora*, which talks *Wolof*, is not tuned in the same way as the Malian *Kora*, which expresses itself in *Bambara*. The *Malinke* xylophone of Guinea does not possess the same scale as the *Bantu* xylophone from the equatorial forest; and although the *Fulani* flute has a similar tone to the flute played by Rwandese shepherds, their "language" bears no resemblance.

Despite these local differences, however, the same vast selection of instruments can be found throughout black Africa, ranging from instruments that produce ear-splitting sounds to those that are barely audible. Similarly, musicians everywhere experiment with unusual sonorities because they seek to produce all manner of weird and complex sounds that often strike Western ears as being impure. Metal jingles may be attached to instruments or dried seeds placed in the sound-box to add their dancing rhythms to the music; drums sometimes have snares. All manner of contrivances are used to produce a variety of sounds—muted, nasal, or strident—that are intended to bring the music as close as possible to the actual sounds of nature. At the same time these devices allow more versatile instruments to be made—instruments that are sometimes capable of playing a melodic line with simultaneous percussion accompaniment.

Such idiosyncrasies and variations notwithstanding, most of the musical instruments found in Africa fall into one or another of the classical categories used in the West. Like Western instruments, they can be divided into stringed, wind, and percussion instruments and can quite easily be placed in one of the four main classifications: chordophones (stringed instruments), idiophones (instruments that produce sounds from substances not stretched or altered in any way, as opposed to stringed instruments or drums); aerophones (wind instruments); and membranophones (instruments with one or more stretched skins).

However, to do full justice to the extraordinarily wide range of instruments in black Africa it is advisable to use a slightly more detailed system of classification; that is: stringed instruments; wind and air instruments; keyboard instruments; drums, with or without skins; rhythmic instruments with vibrating bodies (no strings, skins or keys); corporal instruments; other miscellaneous instruments. We shall examine several of these categories in some detail, referring wherever possible to records that illustrate the corresponding instruments.

STRINGED INSTRUMENTS

There are three types of stringed instruments: bowed (fiddles), plucked (harps, lutes, zithers, harp-lutes, harp-zithers) and beaten (musical bows, earth-bows).

BOWED-STRINGED INSTRUMENTS: Fiddles

The best-known of the bowed-stringed instruments is the one-stringed fiddle that is used by West African musicians, particularly in Muslim regions. It is known by various names in the north of Cameroon and Nigeria, in Chad, and throughout almost the entire zone that extends from Lake Chad to Senegal. The *Wolof* of Senegal call it the *Riti*, the *Tukulor Nyanyur* and the *Songhai* and *Djerma* of Niger refer to it as either the *Godie* or *Godje;* elsewhere in black Africa, it is simply the *Hausa violin*.

The sound-box is made of wood or a hemispherical calabash with a nailed skin, usually lizard skin. A single, horse-hair string is attached to a short neck and stretched over a bridge. A hole is made in the sound-box or in the skin to allow the sound to ''escape,'' as the musicians put it. The bow is a curved stick with a horsehair string that is fixed to both ends. Most one-stringed fiddle

Riti—*the one-stringed fiddle of the* Wolof *musicians of Senegal*

players are such gifted musicians that they almost give the impression that the instrument has more than just one string. The timbre recalls that of the violin or viola, or even the cello, depending on the region and the man who made it. The volume of the sound is in proportion to the size of the instrument and the bow is naturally scaled to size.

One-stringed fiddles may be used as solo instruments but are chiefly employed to accompany singers. They provide the favourite accompaniment of *griots* in Niger, northern Nigeria, and the Timbuctoo area of Mali.[1]

In Niger, there is a type of one-stringed fiddle call *Inzad* that is usually reserved for female musicians.[2] It has a wooden neck that is inserted into a half-calabash, covered with goatskin. A small circular opening in the skin, close to the bridge, is the feature that distinguishes the *Inzad* from other instruments of the same type, in particular from the two Senegalese fiddles mentioned above—the *Wolof Riti* and the *Tukulor Nyanyur*. The sound-box of the *riti* is also hemispherical, but is made from the wood of the silk-cotton tree

A one-stringed fiddle played by a woman from Mali

The Musical Instruments

and is covered with lizard skin. The skin is left intact and instead one or two holes are bored in the underside of the sound-box.[3]

But although the one-stringed fiddle is found in many parts of West Africa, Niger is perhaps the country where it is employed to the best advantage. The musicians of Niger can really make the instrument ''speak'' their respective languages with such a wide range of expression and volume that at times they seem to be making a speech to a vast audience and sometimes to be whispering confidences. They frequently make remarkable use of magic harmonic notes, similar to those of the violin.

The resemblance between fiddle music and singing reaches its peak among the *Tamashek* nomads of Niger. Some of their love songs create the distinct impression that voice and instrument are singing absolutely interchangeable phrases in content as well as in form.[4]

The one-stringed fiddle can also have the purely functional role of creating and maintaining a suitable atmosphere for the performance of certain rites. The magical incantations used in *Mauri* and *Djerma* music (Niger) to invoke the genii, Babai or Zatau, are excellent examples of this usage.[5]

It is interesting to note that *Nago* and *Yoruba* musicians (Nigeria or Dahomey) use the *Godie* one-stringed fiddle in modern African dance bands.[6] The fiddle assumes an almost human role in these bands and reproduces speech patterns and inflections note for note. This ''conversation'' between the fiddle and the rest of the orchestra is somewhat reminiscent of the Western concerto.

The most spectacular form of ''talking'' fiddle is found in Ethiopia where it is the favourite instrument of professional musicians who wander from village to village with their ''musical newspaper.'' A strolling musician singing the news to the accompaniment of a *Masengo* fiddle has been recorded.[7]

Instruments of the fiddle variety are rare in the Congo, but we shall conclude this section with the recording of a *Ba-Lari* song that is accompanied by a *Nsambi* fiddle with three strings.[8]

PLUCKED OR BEATEN-STRINGED INSTRUMENTS

Instruments with plucked or beaten strings have a much wider geographical distribution than the previous group of bowed-stringed instruments, and are more varied in kind, for example, one-stringed lutes—the Molo (Senegal) and the *Kuntigi* (Niger); two-stringed and five-stringed lutes; the harp-lute—*Kora* or *Seron* (Guinea); the *Bolon* harp (Dahomey); the bow-lute of the *Bateke* (Congo); the *mvet* harp-zither of southern Cameroon, and others.

The listener cannot fail to be enraptured by the skills of the African musicians who play such instruments and to see them in action is an added pleasure. The playing of a Senegalese *griot* prompted the French musician, Tolia Nikiprowetzky, to exclaim, ''It is marvellous to see how Amadu Coly Sall, using a simple instrument like a one-stringed lute, manages to capture and hold the listener's attention.'' And he continues, ''His feats of instrumental virtuosity are enhanced by the charms of constant modal ambiguity.''[9]

Konde—*two-stringed lute (Upper Volta)*

Lutes

There are several kinds of lute, varying from region to region in name, shape, and number of strings. In Senegal, the lute goes under the general title of *Khalam* and usually has five strings. The *Khalam* is the favourite instrument of certain *griots*. There are four distinct types: the *Diassare,* the *Bappe*, the *Ndere,* and the *Molo.* The latter is a one-stringed lute that can be used in several ways, either as a solo instrument, or to accompany another *Khalam* or a singer,[10] or even a story-teller. The poet, Leopold Sédar Senghor, advocates the use of the *Khalam* to accompany some of his poems.

The *Bussance* of Upper Volta play a two-stringed lute known as the *Konde.* It consists of a half-calabash that is covered with a skin; the neck has metal bells attached to the end so that when the strings are plucked, the bells jingle. The *Konde* belongs to that category of African instruments whose main purpose is to "speak" rather than to sing.[11]

In Niger the most interesting lutes are the *Kuntigi*[12]—a one-stringed lute used by the *Songhai* and the *Djerma,* and a three-stringed lute—the *Teharden,* played mainly by *Tamashek* musicians. A similar three-stringed lute is used by *Mauri* musicians.[13]

The *Kuntigi* is a small lute with a hemispherical calabash sound-box that is covered with skin. The neck is a slender stick whose free end is fitted with a metal disc surrounded by small rings that clash together at the slightest movement of the instrument, thus providing a rhythmic jingling when the musician plays. The tone of the instrument is shrill yet veiled, like most African lutes that have a sound-box covered with skin. This lightly veiled tone can also be heard on the recording of the Senegalese *Khalam Molo,* although the latter has a larger sound-box which gives a deeper, more powerful resonance.

Finally, in northern Nigeria, mainly in the region of Zaria, there is a two-stringed lute called the *Komo.* It is approximately 2 feet, 3 inches long. The strings are made of twisted antelope skin and are plucked with a hippopotamus-hide plectrum. The upper end of the neck is fitted with a rectangular piece of metal with rounded angles. A number of small vibrating rings are fixed around the perimeter.[14]

Zithers

The zither is another instrument with plucked strings but, unlike the lute, it has no neck. Zithers of varying shapes and tones are found in certain parts of Africa and also in Madagascar. Most of the recordings available were made in Rwanda, Dahomey, and, above all, in Madagascar.

The *Inanga* zither from Rwanda consists of an oval-shaped piece of wood that is hollowed out so that it resembles an elongated bowl. The strings are stretched lengthwise along this piece of wood and are held in place by a series of notches at either end. In fact, there is just one long continuous string that is wound from one side to the other alternately in order to form a set of parallel strings whose tension can be regulated by means of the sharp saw-tooth notches.[15]

The *Mahi* of Dahomey play a raft-zither known as the *Toba.* The strings are stretched lengthwise along a rectangular portable raft that is made from woven reeds. The strings are rather unusual because they are not separate additions, but are actually cut and lifted from the reed bark. The *Toba* has no sound-box and consequently, it has a rather feeble tone. Some musicians amplify the sound of the instrument by holding it over an empty receptacle, such as a bucket. In any event, the instrument is held in both hands and the strings are plucked with the thumbs.[16]

Malagasy zithers are of particular interest. The construction and evolution of the instruments themselves and the music they produce, or are capable of producing, merit special attention. Of the two Malagasy zithers that have been recorded, the *Valiha* is perhaps more interesting than the *Lokanga Voatavo.*

Inanga *zither (Burundi)*

The *Lokanga Voatavo* zither is composed of a number of strings stretched along a stick, one end of which is inserted into an open-bottomed calabash that acts as a sound-box. The stick itself is decorated with intricate carvings and the free end is shaped like a fishtail. In the recording of the *Lokanga Voatavo*, we have chosen as our example two zithers that can be heard accompanying the voices of the musicians.[17]

The *Valiha* is by far the most widespread instrument found on the island of Madagascar; it might even be called the national instrument. It usually consists of a bamboo tube with strings stretched longitudinally around the circumference. The length of the tube varies between 1 foot, 6 inches and 4 feet, 6 inches. Bamboo strings are sometimes used, but nowadays most Malagasy musicians prefer metal strings, which increase the limited volume of the instrument whose sound-box is of very small dimension. The bamboo-stringed zither is idiochordic, that is, the strings are not external additions, but rather, thin strips raised from the body of the instrument.

This type of *Valiha* is made by cutting a length of bamboo with a node at each end. A number of incisions are made along the entire length of the soft outer bark of the tube in order to produce a series of very narrow strips. These are carefully detached from the body of the instrument except at the two ends where they are left attached to the nodes. The whole instrument is then left to dry in the sun. When it is ready, the *Valiha* is tuned by inserting two small bridges under each string. The distance between the bridges can be regulated to produce different notes.

But, as we have already mentioned, this type of "classical" *Valiha* is becoming rare in Madagascar; its place is being taken by instruments made from more modern materials that are more resistant and offer a louder sonority. The *Valiha* is not restricted to the use of village musicians who play traditional music, but is also played by young musicians who have been trained in the Western school.[18] Far from despising the *Valiha,* the younger generation of musicians regard it as a national instrument whose possibilities have not yet been fully explored; and they consider it their duty to foster its future development. One young Malagasy musician recently invented a "chromatic" *Valiha* with 38 strings[19] whose musical potentiality is much greater than that of the traditional instrument, which normally has a maximum of 20 strings.

A Malagasy playing the Valiha *or tubular zither*

The Musical Instruments

Harps

The harp family is represented in certain areas of Central and West Africa. African harps are used chiefly to accompany singers. The number of strings varies from one locality to another and even from one individual maker to another. The most widely used model in Central Africa is the bow-harp which may have one single string (among the *Fang* of Gabon) or ten or so strings (among the *Isongo* or the *Mbaka* of the Congo).

The one-stringed bow-harp is frequently used in quite a remarkable fashion; as well as playing a melodic accompaniment, it simultaneously acts as a percussion instrument. The musician achieves this effect by alternately plucking the string and tapping out the rhythm on the sound-box.[20]

The *Senufo* use one-stringed harps made from large, trisected calabashes that are covered with skins. They have a long curved neck that is finished off with a metal disc, surrounded with metal rings that produce rhythmic rattling sounds.[21]

There are several varieties of bow-harp in Chad. The *Massa* of Western Mayo-Kebbi have a four-stringed version, the *Dilla,* while in Muslim communities, there are musicians who use a five-stringed bow-harp, the *Kinde,* which is placed laterally with the strings parallel to the ground.[22]

The *Ngombi* is another bow-harp that is composed of some ten strings; it is found mainly in the Central African Republic. It provides a much fuller accompaniment for songs and several excellent recordings exist.[23]

A *Wombi* or eight-stringed harp has been recorded among the *Pongwe* of Gabon[24] to accompany a song used in the healing of a sick person. A woman who is a professional healer practises the *abandji* method by which she can transform herself into a supernatural being in order to see into the next world. Thus she is able to find out how to select the barks and leaves that enter into the composition of the baths that are to be administered to the patient. The *Wombi* harp is the medium which leads the woman's spirit into the land of the sirens. The head of this harp is often carved in the image of Ditsuna, the Goddess of Day.

On similar lines is a sacred harp that was also recorded in Gabon.[25] Members of the *Bwiti,* a secret society for the men of the *Bahumbu* tribe in Gabon, gather in the forest to sing the praises of the sacred harp and to address their prayers to it. The sequence begins with a prelude that is played with outstanding virtuosity on the harp. Then, the priest of the sect sings the words of praise; these words are repeated after him by the congregation:

"Oh harp, hewn one night from the wood of the budzinga and the bukuka trees by the bunyenga spirit and the Sky God, grant that we in this country may receive the strength and wisdom of the crocodile, through the intermediary of the bukuka . . . "

This example of the deification of the harp illustrates the remarks made on page 20 concerning the relationship between musical instruments, genii, and

A musician from Northern Nigeria playing an eight-stringed harp

The Musical Instruments

Description of a journey sung by **Massa** *musicians (Chad) to the accompaniment of* three **Dilla** *four-stringed harps*

men. Through the agent of music, the genii confer supernatural powers upon the instrument. In this case, however, the harp has an even more important role; it is not merely the vehicle through which the power of the genii is transmitted to man, but is the actual embodiment of the genii and their power.

We must also mention the forked harp, an example of which has been recorded among the *Baule* of the Ivory Coast.[26] It consists of a forked branch across which five strings are stretched. A half-calabash situated at the join of the fork acts as a resonator. In this recording, the harp is used to accompany a drinking song whose infectious gaiety is apparent, even though the lyrics may be incomprehensible. This is a typical example of *Baule* polyphonic technique that consists of a melodic line that is sung simultaneously on two parallel thirds.

The *Bolon* is a large, three-stringed harp which used to be featured in military parades.[27]

However, these lutes, zithers, and harps that have their counterparts in Western music are by no means the most outstanding members of the plucked-stringed instrument family in black Africa. The composite instruments that

Loma *harp (Liberia)*

The Musical Instruments

combine the different features of these instruments are much more remarkable, such as the *Kora,* a harp-lute from West Africa, and the *Mvet,* a harp-zither that is found mainly in Central Africa.

The *Kora*[28] is one of the most beautiful musical instruments in the whole of black Africa, both visually and aurally. It consists basically of a sound-box, a neck, a large bridge, and 21 strings. The sound-box is a large half-calabash over which a skin is stretched. A hole is cut in the convex part and its contour is carefully decorated. This hole that "allows the sounds to escape naturally" corresponds to the sound hole of the Western lute. Sometimes the entire circumference of the sound-box is decorated, but this is by no means a general rule. A long, cylindrical, wooden neck is inserted into the sound-box. The strings are attached to the end that extends some 1½ inches beyond the sound-box and are fixed at 21 different points to the other end (the neck proper) by means of leather rings that are spaced out along its length. These rings slide along the neck in order that the strings can be held at the required tension for the tuning of the instrument. The bridge, approximately 8 inches high and 1 to 2 inches wide, has ten notches on one side and eleven on the other. The bridge and neck form two sides of a triangle that is completed by the strings that are stretched between them. It is basically this string-feature that places the *Kora* in the harp category. However, because it has a neck it must also be considered a lute. It is therefore more correct to refer to it as a harp-lute. Because the bridge divides the strings into two separate rows, ten on one side and eleven on the other, the *Kora* is actually a double harp. As a finishing touch, the musicians usually fix a round metal disc on top of the bridge. The small rings that are attached to the perimeter of the disc are intended to rattle at the slightest movement. This creation of impure sounds is a feature that we have already mentioned elsewhere.

In ascending order, the notes of the *Kora* are: F—C—D—E—G—Bb—D—F—A—C—E (left hand) and F—A—C—E—G—Bb—D—F—G—A (right hand). However, in spite of the theoretical accuracy of these notes, each one may in practice be a comma higher or lower; this fact often leads Europeans to imagine that the instrument is out of tune. It should be noted that the above mentioned scale is the tuning of the Senegalese *Kora,* as adopted by the School of Arts in Dakar. In Mali and in Guinea where the instrument originated, the tuning is not necessarily the same and is even further removed from the scale of Bach.

In Guinea, there is also a 19-stringed *Kora* called the *Seron.* In all other respects, the instruments are identical and are played in a similar manner. Some excellent recordings of the *Seron* are available. We would like to single out the solos played by an authentic *griot* from the Kankan region of Guinea, a *griot* who ably demonstrates the resources of the instrument.[29] This is purely instrumental music of a very high quality and although the musician knows absolutely nothing about American jazz, it is hard to listen to his playing without being reminded of Negro-American music, notably the Modern Jazz Quartet.

How to hold the five-stringed harp from the Central African Republic

The Musical Instruments

The music of Mamadi Dyubate—a name more typical of the *griot* caste would be hard to find—is not unique in this repect, but we would still hesitate to cite this as proof of the African origins of jazz.

The *Kora* itself is found in a geographical area which includes Guinea, Gambia, Senegal, and southern Mali. Numerous recordings exist of the *Kora* as a solo instrument, as an accompaniment to a singer, and as part of an orchestra. As a solo instrument, it may be heard on a record issued in connection with the First World Festival of Negro Arts in Dakar (April 1966)[30]. As an example of a song with *Kora* accompaniment, we would cite a song in praise of Sundiata, the legendary Emperor of Manding.[31] Like all the other pieces on this particular record, it was made in Paris during a visit of Keita Fodeba's African Ballet Company and it is performed by a *griot* called Dieli Magan. Some purists have shown a certain scepticism about the authenticity of this music, which could in some ways be described as "export art" that is presented by a company that was specifically formed to appear on the music hall stage. However, it must be remembered that the aim of Keita Fodeba and his African Ballets was to promote a mixture of traditional musical and choreography and the modern dance music and dance forms that were currently evolving in contemporary Africa. To omit either of these aspects would not give a balanced picture of Africa. For this very reason, both records made by this company[32] and the variety that they offer are of genuine interest and importance. The over-westernized music of some of the pieces, such as the "Trio Melody Tam-Tam," may not necessarily appeal to all tastes, but the authenticity of the traditional music that is played by the genuine *griots* in the company cannot be question.

Solos and accompaniment to singers are not the only uses of the *Kora*; it can also be found in orchestras or in instrumental duets—with a balaphon for instance.[33] In orchestral ensembles, two *Koras* may be heard with drums, accompanying a singer and a mixed choir.[34] The *Kora*'s effectiveness as an accompaniment to the human voice is perhaps best illustrated in the songs of the late Guinean singer, Konde Kuyate, one of the greatest women *griots* of black Africa. This accompanying role of the *Kora* is shown to particular advantage in the "Song of Siraba"[35] and in the sublime "La illah ila Allah." This song of praise, "There is no god but God," is one of the most beautiful examples of traditional African music and Konde Kuyate's interpretation enhances its beauty and depth of meaning.[36] A discreet yet effective accompaniment, consisting of a single phrase that the *Kora* repeats incessantly throughout the piece, sets off the pure, persuasive development of the vocal theme, "There is no god but God." If the melody were transcribed it would be in 6/8 time which gives the whole piece a calm composure that seduces the ear from the first few notes. The *Kora* heard in this recording has some metal strings, and although their crystalline notes may not be "accurate" in the Western sense, they are in perfect harmony with the powerful voice of the singer and sustain the voice with an unflagging rhythm. The voice states the theme and then improvises upon it in an utterly enchanting manner.

We have already described the *mvet* harp-zither in the chapter dealing with the African musician (see page 29) and so we will at this point merely remind the reader that it is an instrument with plucked strings. A detailed description of the instrument has been given by the Cameroonian musicologist, Eno Belinga, in his book, *Littérature et musique populaire en Afrique noire* (Popular Literature and Music in Black Africa).[37] As we mentioned previously, the repertoire of the *mvet* consists mainly of epic or lyric stories of cosmogonic dimensions. A knowledge of these tales is indispensable to any non-African who wishes to understand African Negroes.

The *mvet* plays a primordial role in the art of relating these legends. The introductory music played by the musician-narrator-dancer on the *mvet* elicits silence from the assembled listeners. The instrument accompanies the entire story and provides musical interludes when the weary narrator wishes to take a few minutes rest. These interludes, in fact, reveal that the musician attributes the same degree of importance to the music as to the story and treats them as equals. He shouts to the crowd of listeners who are hanging on to his every word, "Men, women, brothers, and sisters—what are your ears listening to?" As if one man, the audience roars back, "They are listening to the *mvet*." Then, the harp-zither becomes the centre of attention and as soon as it is begun to be played, it is joined by an impromptu rhythm section, consisting of an empy bottle that is struck with a large iron nail and with one or more wicker rattles. Although the *mvet's* musical possibilities are limited, it largely compensates for this by its personality and the importance it has vis-à-vis the audience.

We have already quoted an extract from one of these stories with *mvet* accompaniment (see page 29),[38] but we thought that it would be interesting to give the translation of another epic from south Cameroon, the tale of Engonezok. Mr. Eno Belinga introduces the record in these words: "A brilliant interpretation which gushes forth among the enraptured audience like an impetuous torrent into a valley. Everyone is hanging on the lips of the zither-toucher, whose tall black silhouette stands out against the dark background of the hut, enveloped in the mysterious black veil of night. Osomo the *mbom-mvet* sings and declaims the noble deeds of the race of Ekan-Nna-Mebe'e."[39] Here is the translation of the recorded extract of the epic:

My tale will not be confined to the mere dispute
Between a citizen of Engonezok and the inhabitants of Ntui;
For there is a far more memorable deed
And I shall now tell you what occurred at Engonezok.
Listen carefully! As you know, it all started
When Nnomongan began to sound his horn
At the hour when the birds, the messengers of dawn,
Burst into song. Nnomongan was in the courtyard.

He swore by all the dead and blew his horn.
As soon as the sound of the horn was heard
The woman who was the wife of Ondo
Felt sharp pains and pangs in her belly.
The wife of Medan felt the same atrocious convulsions,
And the wife of Meye-me-Ngi in turn was seized by the same agony.
Prostrate, racked with the pangs of childbirth
The three wives cried out in their nameless pain.
Suddenly—one!—the wife of Ondo
Gave birth to a male child;
And—two!—the wife of Medan
Gave birth to a male child;
And—three! The wife of Meye-me-Ngi
Gave birth to a male child.
And so it happened that, at almost the same moment,
Three male children were born in Engonezok.
A few minutes later,
Just after the birth of these children,
Nnomongan, the man who initiates into the Mysteries,
Was quite amazed to hear in the clear morning:
"Tu-gu-du-gu-du-gu-du-gu":
The tom-tom announcing its happy news;
Ondo, the father of one of the three children,
Was telling everyone, with beat of drum,
Of the spectacular birth of his son.
Then the tom-tom played the signature tune
Which was Ondo's motto and crest:
"Without nephew or maternal uncle,
Ondo trembles, Ondo rejoices, Ondo is full of joy
And his wife, the daughter of Ndongo,
Radiant as the full scarlet moon,
Has just given birth to a male child."
Nnomongan was still listening when a second tune
Was heard on the drum:
"Medan, with insolence on my brow,
Seated like a lord on my throne of valour and bravery,
Twisted like a knot, Medan
The grandson of Ekan-Nna-Me be'e,
Superior to all, for fortune and I are one,
My wife, beautiful as a lake,
Bright and refreshing as spring water,
Has just given birth to a male child."
Nnomongan was perplexed; and just then
A third signature tune was heard on the drum:

Kora *harp-lutes (Senegal)*

'Tu-gu-du-gu-du-gu-du-gu-du.
Since he elected to live in these parts
To the east of his fields and his lands,
Friendless, unloved by a living soul,
Meye-me-Ngi, who inherited a tree-trunk
From his father, floating on the abyss of life,
On the crest of the wave where the electric fish swims
From whence one fine day he drew forth
A goodly supply of sabres and machettes,
My wife has just given birth to a male child.
Tu-gu-du-gu-kpwo!''
Nnomongan, his heart beating with terror, leapt up
And, after putting into his game bag the mysterious stone
Which he had gone to seek in the abode of the dead,
Went straight to Ondo's house and asked him:
''Why are you beating your tom-tom?''
''My wife,'' replied Ondo, ''has just given birth
To a male child.''
''Take me to this child at once; it's an order.''
When they got inside the hut
They saw the baby crying, ''Nyan-nyan-nyan-nyan.''
Turning to the mother Nnomongan said,
''Woman, you are indeed beautiful, daughter of Ndongo,
You are as radiant as the full scarlet moon.
May I look upon your illustrious baby?''
Nnomongan took the illustrious baby in his arms,
And turning to the father, he said,
''You wished that your wife would never bear
A child in her womb; didn't you know
That one day an illustrious descendant would
Be born in Engonezok? And today you dare pretend
That this child is yours. . . I tell you,
You are an insult to our race.'' Then Ondo
Excused himself and said,
''Forgive me, it's true, I did say such things.''
But suddenly Nnomongan put the baby in his bag
And drew out a copper jewel: at that moment
The father of the child took fright and shouted,
''Nnomongan, where are you taking my son?''
As though by magic, the shadow of Nnomongan vanished
And disappeared like a dream.
''Tu-gu-du-gu-du-gu-du-gu-du.''
Ondo set off in pursuit
But could not seize the impalpable shadow of Nnomongan.

Mvet *harp-zither (Cameroon)*

The Musical Instruments

He crossed the yard, but saw no-one.
Ondo went up to the sky,
Looked in the clouds and still saw no-one,
Nnomongan was already far away in the East,
In the spheres where the sun lights up each day.

Nnomongan went to Medan Endon's house.
He stole the child and took it off in his bag.
Then he went to Meye-me-Ngi. He stole the third baby
And took it off in his bag. Nnomongan,
The master of initiations, went up to the sky
And then went home. He entered, closed the door
Nine times with padlocks, crossed a dark room
And came to the magic bath
Where the Mysteries bathed; he took the three babies
And put them into the bath: and then, once more, he sounded his horn.
After which, he made an invocation:"Oh ancestors,
The power of mortals has its bounds. Oh fathers,
Meme'e m'Ekan, Ngeme-Ekan, Oyono-Ekan,
The three babies are waiting in the bath of Mysteries.
Tell me now, who on earth is going to keep an eye on them?''

The *mvet* harp-zither is found mainly in south Cameroon, in the north of Gabon and Congo-Brazzaville, and in the Central African Republic. It is not solely used to accompany epic narrations but may also be used simply to accompany recitatives or songs.[40] Another type of harp-zither, found in the Congo and known as the *Mboko,* is unusual because instead of a sound-box that is made from a half-calabash, it has a sort of small, plaited-bamboo mat that is level with the bridge. Finally, there are harp-zithers with no sound-box at all, such as those sometimes made by the Pygmies of the tropical forest.[41] The *mvet* of the *Fang* tribe (south Cameroon and Gabon) usually has four strings. They are raised from the palm stalk that composes the body of the instrument and they pass over a bridge that is fixed half-way between the two ends of the stalk. The ensemble of the strings is thus divided into two sets, providing four notes for each hand. These notes sometimes have specific names, as for example, those given to the sounds produced by the *Fang mvet* that is tuned to accompany the epic of Akoma Mba. The Western notes that are indicated in brackets are those that come closest to the actual sounds, but they are nevertheless only approximate.

left hand: Ekang Na (E)—Na Mongom (D)—Evini Tsang (C)—Akoma
    Mba (A)
right hand: Ntuntumu Mfulu (C)—Engwang Ondo (B or Bb)—Medang
    Boro (A)—Medza Motugu (F).

Bow-lutes

Another member of the stringed instrument family of black Africa is the bow-lute. A bow-lute has a sound-box with several wooden bows imbedded in it; these hold the strings. The bow-lute is among the oldest known traditional instruments; its existence is mentioned in various travel journals dating back to the sixteenth century. It is quite certainly the ancestor of the *Ngombi* bow-harp from the Central African Republic and other similar harps. In its most developed form, where the bows are not separated but joined by raffia links, it certainly recalls the shape of a harp. The only difference is that the plane of the strings is not perpendicular to the top of the sound-box. The bow-lute is commonly used by forest walkers in maintaining a regular rhythm and very often it accompanies the incantations of magicians, especially medicine-men.[42]

The earth-bow—a curious voice that seems to emanate from the earth

Musical Bows

There are several types of musical bow in black Africa. Those that have been recorded so far are the earth-bow, mouth-bow, and resonator-bow.

The earth-bow consists of a flexible wooden pole planted in the ground. A string is stretched from the upper end to a small plank or piece of bark that covers a hole in the ground. The hole acts as a resonator. When the string is plucked or struck, the sound apparently emerges from the bowels of the earth. This explains why it is much used in magic.[43]

The mouth-bow is a wooden bow with one string stretched between the two ends and is struck with a stick. The musician places the string between his parted lips so that his mouth acts as a resonator. The sound can be amplified or diminished by opening or closing the mouth. The pitch is varied by means of a touch that is moved along the string with the left hand.[44] Sometimes, a musician will sing and simultaneously accompany himself on the mouth-bow in a curious kind of dialogue in which he takes both parts.[45]

The resonator-bow is a variation on the mouth-bow, however, it has the addition of a calabash resonator that is placed in the middle of the bow. In Rwanda, where it is fairly widespread, it is called *Munahi*. The instrument is also found in Dahomey and is call the *Tiepore*. The same instrument in Madagascar is known as the *Jejolava* bow.[46]

WIND AND AIR INSTRUMENTS

This group of instruments is fairly well-represented in black Africa, although some of them are limited to a very narrow geographical area. Whistles, *mirlitons,* flutes, trumpets or horns, clarinets, and oboes are all played in one or more parts of the continent. One general remark applies to this group; unlike instruments of other categories, absolutely no attempt is made to modify their timbre. The curious timbre of the *mirliton*—thanks to which it plays an important role in music and in society—is not due to any intentional acoustic experimentation. The sonority of the flute is universal. The *alghaita* happens to have the timbre of an oboe and no artifice is employed to alter it in any way. Simlarly, most horns and trumpets emit completely unaltered sounds, in contrast with lutes which are often equipped with jingles, or with certain percussion instruments equipped with resonators. These horns and trumpets are usually beautifully carved and often rank as genuine works of sculpture.

Mirlitons

Mirlitons are found in a good many African communities, either as children's toys or as instruments for the use of adults in certain rituals. The *mirliton* which features in the ritual ceremonies of the *Dan*—a tribe which straddles the western frontier of the Ivory Coast with Liberia—has attracted the attention of many investigators and has been recorded several times. It consists of a hollow

Necked whistle (Dahomey)

The Musical Instruments

bird bone, one end of which is stopped with a spider's web membrane. The other end, the part held in the mouth, is left open. When the player talks or sings with this *mirliton* in his mouth, the membrane vibrates and "masks" his voice. In other words, it is an "acoustic" mask. The *Baegbo* mask is comprised of five young men playing *mirlitons* of this type. They perform as a unit which is considered as a single mask and, although it is not the usual type of mask that is worn, women and girls are not permitted to see it. Hence the *Baegbo* is only formed at night and outside of the village. In former times, this *mirliton*-mask wielded enormous power. It was the vehicle of punishment for any man or woman who had broken the law or failed in his or her duty to the community. Today the *Baegbo* is usually just a means of entertainment for young people.[47]

Whistles

Whistles may be used to mark the rhythm for dancing, but as each whistle produces only one note, their use is somewhat limited. Sometimes, however, they are formed into orchestras. Each whistle plays its own note at a given moment in the ensemble in order to produce a melodic line. The complexity of this type of music is quite astonishing. The whistle may also be used concurrently with the human voice; the musician sings a tune that is punctuated at regular intervals by the sound of the whistle. This is a common practice in Pygmy music.[48]

Flutes

The flute is always a delightful instrument and the music of the African flute is particularly accessible to non-African ears, mainly because it has a universal timbre. One of the three varieties of flute—vertical, oblique, or transverse (panpipes are unknown in Africa)—is the constant companion of every shepherd[49] and cowherd. Whether in solo or duet,[50] they produce a variety of charming melodies that may be slow or fast and light, philosophical meditations or satirical tunes.[51] The number of finger-holes varies between two and six in different regions. The *Fali* of northern Cameroon, for example, use a vertical, notched flute with four finger-holes called *Feigam*.[52] But without any doubt the most beautiful flute music is that of the *Fulani* shepherds who achieve exquisite results with an instrument that is simply a length of reed.[53] Flute duets are often seen as a symbolic representation of the couple, the genesis of life, and the music they produce is considered symbolic of the fruit of their union.[54] Consequently, there are male and female flutes, the latter generally being smaller in size. As in any marriage, there are times when man and wife disagree. An argument may then ensue between the male and female flutes, but instead of bittersweet words, there is music, which despite the storm, is no less charming to the ear.[55]

Finally, as in the West, the flute can be used in instrumental ensembles. It can usually be distinguished from the other instruments by its characteristic timbre, making it the most universal instrument in all African music.[56]

Ivory transverse horns (Ivory Coast)

The Musical Instruments

Trumpets and Horns

In different parts of the continent, trumpets, horns, or even elephant tusks are also used to provide musical sounds. Most of these trumpets are animal horns, but in some areas they are made from wood or metal; such a trumpet is the *Kakaki* played by *Hausa* musicians from Niger, Nigeria, north Cameroon and Chad. The *Babembe* of the Congo make trumpets in human likeness; they are huge instruments with a dorsal mouthpiece and an open base. Most wind instruments have a very limited register, restricted to one or two notes. In Dahomey, the *Berba* use transverse horn trumpets that have a lateral opening through which the player blows; a hole at the opposite end can be stopped with the index finger.[57] The *Baule* of the Ivory Coast use the *Awe* trumpet as the voice of the male genie, Goli, when he emerges from the forest during the funeral of a farmer.[58] A *Broto* trumpet orchestra (Central African Republic) comprised of four small horn trumpets and eight large wooden ones has been recorded.[59] This is initiation music which sounds not unlike jazz, being slightly reminiscent of the brass section of Duke Ellington's orchestra, for example. It begins with an introduction, a kind of call that is played twice in succession by a small trumpet and is answered by the whole orchestra. Then, the other trumpets make their entry one by one and play together for a while. A melodic line is achieved by the dexterous combination of the single notes that are produced by each instrument. A high-pitched trumpet announces the end of the piece; then, the entire orchestra answers this solo. Finally, a second call, followed by an ensemble response, brings the piece to a close.

The *Truta* trumpets of the *Dan* (in *Dan* language *tru* means trumpet) are similar to the Congolese ones mentioned earlier; both types are made of ivory. The *Truta* are transverse trumpets and once again they perform in an ensemble where the music consists of the successive emission of the trumpets' respective notes. An orchestra of this kind, composed of six transverse trumpets (five of which are different in size) has been recorded.[60] The lowest and the highest trumpets produce two notes each, the rest produce a single note. The dancers who encircle the musicians sing certain tunes, pronounce names, or recite proverbs to inspire a particular piece of music; subsequently, the trumpets begin to play this music as though in answer to the dancers' invitation. In former times, these orchestras of ivory trumpets belonged exclusively to chieftains and were used to play court music in their honour. They were also used to encourage warriors going into battle or to greet them on their victorious return.

Another trumpet orchestra has been recorded among the *Babembe* in the Congo. This orchestra consists of four trumpets in human likeness, representing four people: father, mother, son, and daughter. The first three are held vertically, the fourth horizontally. The music played by this orchestra is connected with ancestor worship.[61]

Oblique flutes (Niger)

The Musical Instruments

Bamileke carved ivory horn (Cameroon)

There are numerous other varieties of trumpet in West Africa. Generally speaking, they are made from calabash. In northern Cameroon and south-west Chad, for instance, there is a trumpet known as the *Hu-hu*. It can be used either as a proper musical instrument (the musician blows into the mouthpiece and uses his lips as a reed to produce sounds) or merely as a loudspeaker. The *Hu-hu*[62] consists of a long tube attached to a bell; both are made of calabash. The player frequently holds it in one hand and shakes a calabash rattle with the other, but this is not a general rule.

The calabash bell is sometimes attached to a horn or wooden tube. This type of trumpet, which may be vertical or transverse, is sometimes fitted with a sort of appendix, a small supplementary tube which communicates with the main tube at the level of the mouthpiece. When the instrument is played, this supplementary tube is alternately stopped and opened with one finger. In addition, the main tube may be equipped with one or more *mirlitons*—yet another example of the quest for timbre which is so characteristic of African music.

Among the *Tupuri* of south-west Chad, a region known as Mayo-Kebbi, trumpet orchestras made up of up to ten wind instruments of various types may be heard at harvest time.[63]

Kakaki

The *Kakaki* is a man-made trumpet whose chief exponents are the *Hausa* people of Niger, northern Nigeria, Chad, and the north of Cameroon. It is a tin trumpet which can measure up to 9 feet in length. It consists of two distinct parts that are slotted together: a conical bell, some 4–6 inches in diameter and about 1 foot, 6 inches high, and a cylindrical body, approximately 1 inch in diameter, widening out to 2 to 4 inches at the mouthpiece. Apart from its remarkable size, the *kakaki* also possesses an impressive, shattering timbre. Its limited resources prohibit its use as a solo instrument (it produces barely two notes, a fifth apart) but its majestical tone is employed to augment orchestral ensembles. With a few rare exceptions, the *Hausa* utilize wind instruments exclusively in honour of dignitaries, in particular high-ranking officials of the traditional government. The traditional government of Nigeria has not been abolished or replaced by new national institutions; the *Hausa* territory in the north is still divided into Emirates, ruled by Emirs. The Sultan is senior to all the Emirs and the band that plays in his honour is composed of the best musicians in the country. The fanfare sometimes played to salute an Emir at dawn also acts as a reveille for the rest of the population.[64] The composition of these bands varies, of course, but the ''Fanfare for the Sultan of Sokoto'' (Nigeria) with its three *kakaki*, three *alghaita* (oboes with a single reed), and drums[65] is fairly typical.

Babembe *horns in human likeness (Congo)*

Animal horn used as a transverse trumpet

The Musical Instruments

Hu-hu *calabash trumpet (North Cameroon)*

A musician from Chad playing a **Hu-hu calabash trumpet**

The Musical Instruments

Alghaita *oboe player*

Alghaita

Most *Hausa* orchestras are composed of two *kakaki*, one *alghaita* and a rhythm section of variable size. The *alghaita* is a conical, collapsible oboe whose two constituent parts are linked by a tiny chain. A metal tube containing the reed is slotted into a wooden body that is covered with leather. The base of the body, which has four finger-holes, widens out into a bell. The reed (which is literally a piece of reed) fits into the upper end of the metal tube that is immediately above a small iron disc soldered to the tube. When the musician places the reed in his mouth, his lips rest against this disc, which hermetically seals the air reservoir that is constituted by his mouth. Such a technique is aimed at producing a continuous sound that does not depend on the musician's breathing, but is only interrupted if he so desires. Before beginning to play, he inhales a large mouthful of air and puffs out his cheeks as much as possible. The disc enables him to control the amount of air entering the oboe in order to ensure that the air reservoir never empties; as he plays he continues to breathe in through the nose so that the volume of air in his mouth remains constant. This system enables the *alghaita* to be played without any interruption for hours on end, rather like bagpipes. This characteristic is evident in most *alghaita* recordings.

No less remarkable are its amazingly voluble improvisations which, because of the piercing tone of the instrument, are set off to advantage in orchestral ensembles. The *alghaita* always manages to make itself heard through even the most deafening percussion. A *Hausa* praise song in honour of

An orchestra of flutes, alghaita, kakaki, and drums

Millet-stalk clarinets

the Djermakoy (*Djerma* king) has been recorded in the palace courtyard in Dosso (Niger) in the presence of the Djermakoy himself.[66] Like all dignitaries of the *Hausa* or *Djerma* societies, the Djermakoy has *griots* attached to his court and this song, accompanied by an *alghaita*, is performed by one of them.

Naturally though, the possibilities of the *alghaita* and the virtuosity of the black artists who play it are best heard in ensembles. The *alghaita* is often grouped with three drums and manages to take the preponderant role, whether in improvisations of a rare variety or in dance music.[67] The *alghaita* that is played by the *Djerma* is larger than that of other tribes, and consequently, it produces a deeper, more powerful sound.[68] The virtuosity of the players of this African oboe is such that they even manage, because of a system of phonetic equivalences, to send messages with the instrument that can be decoded by the initiated.

Clarinets

There are two types of clarinet worth noting, namely the *Fulani* clarinet, *Bobal,* and an idioglottic clarinet, which is known as *Papo* in Dahomey and *Bumpa* in Upper Volta. The *Bobal* is merely a millet stalk with a slit at one end.[69] The *Bumpa* clarinet that is played by the *Bussance* in Upper Volta is identical to the *Papo* of the *Dendi* (Dahomey) and is also a millet stalk, but has a vibrating reed at one end and a lateral hole at the other. A small calabash that is pierced with several holes is placed at each end of the stalk. The column of air in the stalk vibrates when the musician alternately inhales and exhales through the loose reed; he simultaneously stops or opens the lateral hole with his thumb. The two calabashes modify slightly the timbre and volume of the instrument. Although it is technically a clarinet, it does sound rather like a saxophone. The possibilities of the *Papo* are such that it may some day be able to broaden its horizons; at the present time, these are rather limited. The music of the *Papo* is of astonishing beauty and simplicity.[70]

This clarinet is known as Bumpa *in Upper Volta and* Papo *in Dahomey.*

KEYBOARD INSTRUMENTS

Two keyboard instruments are used in black African music: the *Sanza*, an instrument with plucked keys, and the xylophone whose keys are struck.

Some musicologists have claimed that the *Sanza* is "the only invention that can be attributed to the African Negroes." We shall not be quite so categorical since our purpose is not to discuss the origins of African musical instruments. We shall merely point out that the *Sanza* is found in various far-flung parts of the continent. It is known by a number of different names, but even though its external appearance varies, the principle and the technique that is used are invariable. It is usually a rectangular wooden parallelopiped about 9 inches long, 5 inches wide and 2 inches high. These are the minimum dimensions and there are much larger *Sanzas* that usually provide the bass notes in instrumental ensembles. The sound-box may be in a single block—a piece of hollowed-out wood with an opening at the front or the back that acts as the sound hole—or in several pieces of wood, bamboo, or palm stalk that are joined together.

A number of keys made of narrow strips of bamboo, bark, or metal are fixed to the sound-board and attached to the back of the bridge, either separately or all together. The tips of the keys, which are suspended over the sound hole, are weighted down with beads of resin. The tuning of the instrument varies from one tribe to another, and is obtained by varying the length of the keys. The *Sanza* is held in both hands and the tips of the keys are plucked with the thumbs or index fingers. It produces a pleasing sound whose tone depends on the material of which the keys are made and the amount of resin stuck on the tips. It is sometimes referred to as "the little African piano". 10, 16, 20, 26, and sometimes even 30 keys afford musical possibilities that can be enlarged by associating several instruments of the same type; two or three *Sanzas* are often played together. The large *Sanzas* are classed as percussion instruments with variable sounds and generally have a maximum of five keys.

Sanza, *Sanzi*, *Sanze* and *Sanzo* are variations of the same instrument. It is also called *Likembe* or *Gibinji* in the Congo; *Timbili* by the *Vute* (or *Babute*) of Cameroon; and *Deza* by the *Lemba* of the Transvaal in South Africa. In Upper Volta, the *Bussance* know it as the *Kone*. Other versions may also well exist.

The *Sanza* is above all an instrument used for relaxation and recreation. Many nightwatchmen in the commercial areas of African towns play the *Sanza* to make the long night hours "pass more quickly." It is also a popular instrument for people making long journeys on foot through the forest and could be termed, "the walker's friend."[71] It can be played as a solo instrument or can accompany vocal or choral music; it is also found in orchestras. There is a beautiful recording of the *Kone Sanza* (made in the *Bussance* region of Upper Volta)[72] that could almost be taken for modern jazz; the successive rhythms, the phrasing and polyphony, even the tone of the instrument, could be compared to the vibraphone playing of someone like Milt Jackson. A *Bagandu*

Kone Sanza *(Upper Volta)*

Sanza and xylophone duet and a satirical song with *Sanza* accompaniment (both recorded in the Central African Republic)[73] give some idea of the various combinations obtainable with this little instrument.

But the *Sanza* is not *merely* an instrument of recreation. In some regions, it has an important symbolic role that cannot be overlooked. The *Lemba*, a *Bantu* tribe from the Transvaal, consider the *Deza Sanza* as a sacred object. It represents the *Lemba* ancestors and enables them to be reincarnated through the medium of dancers, etc. Its physical appearance and the materials from which it is made, as well as the music it plays, are strictly governed by initiation laws that are associated with the python myth. One manifestation of this myth is the *Domba* or python dance, "a fertility rite in which young men and girls fresh

The Musical Instruments

from their respective puberty schools come together to follow a joint course of instruction in preparation for marriage." During the dance, the instructor sings while the novices link arms and dance; they simulate the slow movements of an uncoiling python. In this society, the python is directly linked with female fertility; a sterile woman wears a python skin around her neck and back in the hope of becoming fertile.

This belief arises from a legend that usually runs as follows: "The python took a second wife who did not realize that he was a python. At night, she felt something cold sliding towards her, but when she asked what it was, the python told her to be quiet. In the daytime, she used to go and work in the fields with the first wife. She was curious to see her husband and tried to find pretexts for going back to the village, but the first wife always prevented her. One day, however, she pretended to have forgotten her spade and went back to the village where she saw the python sitting in the men's courtyard, quietly smoking his pipe. He was so furious that she had seen him that he rushed off and disappeared into the depths of Lake Fundudzi. Then the rain stopped falling; the crops withered; a great famine reigned throughout the land and all the streams dried up. The divining bones were consulted and revealed that the disappearance of the python was the cause of the trouble; he wanted his young wife to go and join him at the bottom of Lake Fundudzi. The people were immediately called together and the royal princesses began preparing the ritual beer, *mpambo*. When the *mpambo* was ready, everyone went down to the lake; the men were dancing and playing the *tshikona*, an invocation to the ancestors of the tribe, while the women carried the *mpambo*. The python's wife was hidden in the midst of the crowd and could hear nothing but the sound of the *Tshikona* flutes. When they arrived at the lake, they offered the *mpambo* to the python in propitiation and the young woman, holding the gourd of beer in her arms, went into the water and disappeared into the depths of the lake to join her husband. And the rain began to fall . . ."

This is the reason that each year a young *Lemba* girl must disappear into Lake Fundudzi in the Northern Transvaal in order to join the python and bring rain. As far as we know, the sacrifice still takes place today.

Initiation into the *Domba* rite is, therefore, an event of major importance for the *Lemba* tribespeople. Every initiate spends several months dancing the python dance—a dance that imitates the uncoiling of the python—singing "Tharu ya Mabidighami" ("the python uncoils") and learning the *Domba* laws. Such an initiate thus comes to understand the origin of the myth, "In the beginning mankind and the whole of creation were seated in the belly of the python; one day he spewed them forth."

The *Deza Sanza*, with its 22 keys, contained in a hemispherical calabash resonator, actually represents the whole of creation and mankind that is seated in the python's belly. The striking of the notes to produce sound is truly an act of creation—the birth of a child who cries; the wooden frame represents the women who have come to assist at the birth. Every single component part of the

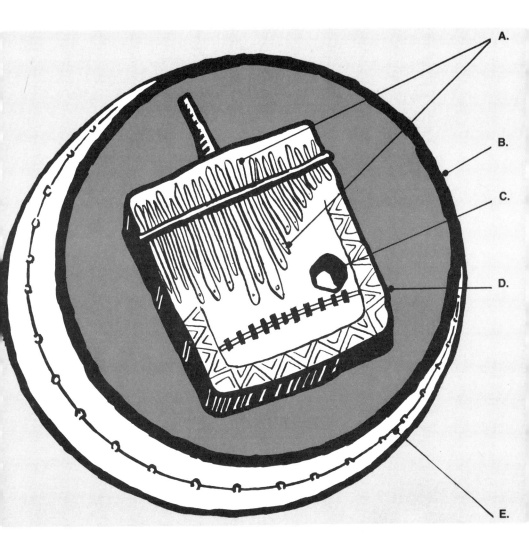

Deza Sanza *of the* Lemba *(Transvaal)*

A. *The keys of the* Sanza *represent the men seated in the python's belly (22 notes).*

B. *Calabash—the womb*

C. *The sound-hole symbolizes the deflowered maiden.*

D. *The* Sanza *fixed inside a calabash; the frame represents the women who have come to help the young woman in labour (to pluck the keys is to create—the sound is the child being born).*

E. *String tied round the calabash representing the python skin encircling the village*

The Musical Instruments

Deza is symbolic: the calabash resonator is the womb; the sound, as we have just explained, is the child that is born; the string that is tied around the calabash represents the python skin that encircles the village; the keys are the people who are seated inside the python—8 men (the high notes), 7 old women represented by copper keys (copper being the metal of the womenfolk—the *Lemba* consider red to be a feminine colour); the hole in the rectangular sound-box is the deflowered maiden, and so on.

So the *Deza Sanza* is a musical instrument that not only represents the creation of sound and the perpetual renewal of the first creation (when the python vomitted), it also reflects the structure and laws of the society; laws which "Mwari," the God-Creator, taught the first men who played the *Deza Sanza*. In short, as far as the *Lemba* are concerned, the *Deza Sanza* is synonymous with life.[74]

Xylophone

There are few African countries in which this instrument does not exist; in some respects it is just as representative of African music as is the drum. The xylophone may be resonated or unresonated, but it invariably has wooden keys that are struck with mallets (also made of wood) with rubber or leather tips. The type of wood varies from region to region; it also depends on the sonority desired; soft, light wood gives a deadened sound, while hard wood renders a crystalline sound. There are virtually no rules as to the choice of material. The number of keys also varies, from three to as many as 17—the number on the xylophone that is used by the *Bapende* (Congo). The simplest form is the leg-xylophone that consists of three or four wooden bars that are placed cross-wise on the outstretched legs of the musician. Leg-xylophone players often sit on a wooden mortar or some other large object that acts as an amplifier. This is common practice in the north of Togo, in the *Kabre* area, where the keys of the xylophone are usually comprised of four or five stalks of dried Palmyra palm.[75]

Log-xylophones are found in the south-west of Cameroon and other parts of Central Africa. Two long banana-tree trunks that are laid on the ground act as supports for some 15 wooden keys. These long keyboards are usually played by two or three musicians and another man, whose task is to supervise the smooth running of the performance, stands facing the musicians and replaces any keys that are accidentally dislodged. The instrument forms part of a traditional dance orchestra, also comprised of *mirlitons,* whistles, drums, and other rhythm instruments. When the dancing is over, the xylophone keys are removed and the banana-tree trunks are put away in a cool place to keep them in good condition until the next performance. The *Azande* of the Central African Republic call this type of xylophone, the *Kponimbo*. There is a recording of the *Kponimbo*, accompanied by a two-headed drum that plays *gbwenlen*, a type of dance music that in this instance is played merely for entertainment.[76]

Log-xylophone (Central African Republic)

Leg and log-xylophones are by no means the best-known examples of this family of instruments. By far the most popular type of xylophone is the *Balaphon*. Portable or otherwise, these xylophones have calabash resonators that vary in size according to the pitch of the notes desired. The resonators are fixed under the keys, which are attached to a rectangular frame by a long piece of string. There is a hole in each calabash that is covered with a *mirliton* and attached with resin. The *mirlitons* may be made from a spider's web, a thin piece of fish or snake skin, or a bat's wing. These *mirlitons* give the *Balaphon* its characteristic timbre, which is quite unlike that of the similar instruments

Senufo xylophones and drums (Ivory Coast)

that one encounters in South American Negro music. The African xylophone is the ancestor of the Latin American marimba; the large xylophone with 17 keys that is used by the *Bapende* in the Congo is called *Madimba*. Such a term leaves no doubt as to the origin of the Latin American instrument. In some countries, *Balaphon* players wear on their arms metal bells whose jingling adds an extra sound to the music.[77]

There is an abundance of xylophone recordings of many kinds, ranging from solo performances to the xylophone orchestras that exist in various regions of black Africa.[78] There are also all sorts of interesting combinations, such as a beautiful example of *Bagandu* music (Central African Republic) with a xylophone and *Sanza* duet; the two instruments blend perfectly and they simultaneously produce unexpected rhythmic effects.[79] Examples of this are an excellent xylophone and *Kora* duet from Senegal[80] and a duet for xylophone and voice that is performed by a blind musician from Upper Volta who is an extraordinary virtuoso and singer.[81]

In some parts of Africa, xylophones were used in divination rites. The xylophone, together with a small wooden drum with no membrane, accompanied the chanting of a fetisher, while he tracked down wrongdoers or healed the sick. Now, *Balaphons* are usually played for entertainment purposes and it is not uncommon to see village squares or town market places filled with large crowds who gather around the *Balaphon* players for the mere pleasure of dancing.

On such occasions, certain tribes of equatorial Africa single out as the main attraction two or three very young girls who dance with all the elegance, grace, and technical ability of confirmed stars. The *mendjang* dance of the

Xylophones with curved keyboards (Upper Volta). The calabashes act as the sound-box of the instrument.

Fang of south Cameroon and north Gabon is a typical example. Confining the leading role to little girls is a reminder that in former times it was mainly the Pygmies—or little people—who were the star performers. Another interesting feature of this dance is the special use of the instrument that "converses" with the dancers. The *mendjang* orchestra of the *Fang* consists of at least four or five xylophones and sometimes percussion instruments are added—single or double iron bells, rattles, etc. The xylophone ensemble forms a keyboard of 30 to 40 wooden keys that cover a range of more than three octaves. The orchestra and dancers are ready and the village square is packed. One of the xylophones, usually played by the group leader, begins with a short prelude. Thus, he requests the audience to be silent and warns the dancers to get ready. After this introduction, a "conversation" begins between the instrument and the dancers, along the lines of the following, which Mr. Herbert Pepper recorded among the *Fang* people of Gabon:[82]

XYLOPHONE:	Hey there, girls!
DANCERS:	Yes!
XYLOPHONE:	Where are you from?
DANCERS:	We are from Endoumsang, from Nseme Nzimi's family. You can tell from his eyes that he is sad and would be capable of dying of hunger right next to a pile of suger cane.
XYLOPHONE:	Aha?
DANCERS:	Aha!
XYLOPHONE:	A poor country . . .?
DANCERS:	Is one where a man must rely on his flocks to live.
XYLOPHONE:	The sin of adultery . . . ?
DANCERS:	You forgive your brother if he steals from you, don't you?
XYLOPHONE:	Cocoa leaves . . . ?
DANCERS:	I made a mat from some this evening.
XYLOPHONE:	An evil place . . . ?
DANCERS:	Is where you never meet the man you love.
XYLOPHONE:	Spinsters' letters . . . ?
DANCERS:	Never mention men.
XYLOPHONE:	Aha?
DANCERS:	Aha!

After this verbal game, the other xylophones join in so that the young dancers can show off their talents. Needless to say, these games have a vast repertoire that range from proverbs of great wisdom to the most trivial events.

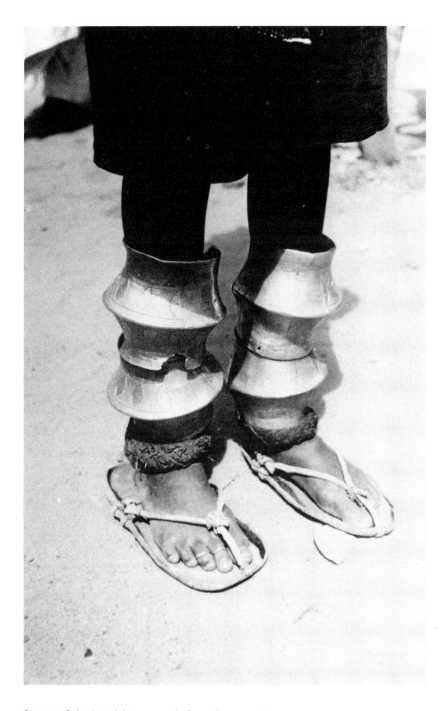

Layers of rhythm rising upwards from the ground

The Musical Instruments

These Guinean xylophones have no calabash resonators to amplify the sound.

Lithophones

Lithophones are a very particular type of instrument and they are limited to certain parts of black Africa, such as the north of Togo and, in quite a different form, in northern Nigeria. A lithophone is a group of basalt stones. When struck, these produce sounds that can be incorporated into a piece of music. The shape and size of the stones vary considerably. In the *Kabre* region of northern Togo, the instrument consists of four or five flat stones that are arranged in star formation on the ground or on a bed of straw. The musician hits them with two stone strikers; the striker that is held in the right hand usually plays the tune, while the other punctuates the musical phrases or taps out the rhythm on the largest stone, which has the deepest or most neutral sound. Every *Kabre* family has its own lithophone, which is usually played by the young boys. Based on the farming cycle, this music has a marked seasonal character. For instance, in the first days of mid-November, the lithophone is played to mark the end of the rainy season and in December, it announces the feast of the millet harvest. The instrument must not be played after the millet harvest. Each agricultural feast has its own particular music that may not be played at any other time. This taboo

Kabre *lithophone (Northern Togo)*

The Musical Instruments

is scrupulously respected because the farming rite is closely connected with the cult of the dead and the dead have the power to fertilize the soil and make rain.[83]

Giant lithophones exist in northern Nigeria, chiefly in the regions of Kano and Jos. These lithophones are composed mostly of groups of rocks that have been found in natural formation. The music they produce is still used in some villages for initiation and circumcision ceremonies or for certain religious ceremonies. As in northern Togo, there is a similar relationship between the lithophone and farming. In and around Nok, the sound of the rocks can be heard before the first harvest of the year. Single girls take seeds and crush them on the large sonorous rocks.

In Kusarha, near northern Cameroon, the lithophone is used as a means of communication with the spirits whose voices can be heard echoing from the caverns in the rocks.

In the past, the main use of the lithophone in northern Nigeria was to warn of an enemy approach in time of war. This was the method used in the nineteenth century to signal the arrival of the *Fulani* horsemen who were advancing across the plain some 3 to 4 miles off and were bringing the Holy War. These days, lithophones are also used to accompany dance music.

The lithophone concludes our inventory of melodic instruments. Drums and other percussion complete this survey of African musical instruments.

DRUMS

It is scarcely necessary to emphasize the importance of drums in African music. These instruments are considered throughout the world to be the most representative African instruments; and for many non-Africans, they are the only ones. The preceding pages have shown the error in such a judgment. Yet, the drum is, without question, the instrument that best expresses the inner feelings of black Africa. These drums possess a vast range of materials, shapes, uses, and taboos. They have remained constant throughout the ages and they are extraordinarily popular throughout the continent. Even outside of Africa, on their long journey of expatriation (during the evil days of slavery and after), they have managed to adapt themselves to conditions of life totally different from those on the black African Continent. They epitomize the real definition of African music—a music that speaks in rhythms that dance. No genuine African music is an exception to this definition and the reason for this fact lies in the omnipresence of drums in the Negro musical world. Even when the drum itself is physically absent, its presence is reflected by hand-clapping, stamping, or the repetition of certain rhythmic onomatopoeias that are all artifices that imitate the drum beat.

But to the Negro, music and speech are often synonymous. Here too, the drum finds its rightful place, a place of honour that enables it to participate in all ceremonies that mark important stages in a man's life (cf. the remarks made on page 10 about the initiation ceremonies of the *Adiukru* of the Ivory Coast).

Baule *percussion (Ivory Coast)*

And even on less solemn occasions, the voice of the drum is employed—to communicate a piece of news or to send a message from one village to another. The art and technique of the drummed message achieve a very high degree of competence. But not all Africans can understand or transmit messages with the aid of a drum; it is a skill that requires a patient apprenticeship.

The instruments that are used and their techniques, as well as the forms of language transmitted, differ from region to region. The *Yoruba* of Dahomey and Nigeria, for example, use a small, two-headed hour-glass drum. The instrument is held under the armpit and is struck with a hammer-shaped stick. Variations in the tension of the skins are obtained by exerting pressure with the forearm on the longitudinal thongs that connect the skins; this gives different sonorities which can reproduce all the tones of speech. This hour-glass drum (*Tama* to the *Wolof*, *Kalengu* to the *Hausa*) sends actual spoken messages; that is, the musician regulates the pressure with his forearm so as to reproduce notes that correspond to the register of the word that he is transmitting. This method

Griots *playing hour-glass drums*

of playing spoken phrases on a drum is particularly appropriate in the case of tonal languages, such as *Yoruba* or certain *Bantu* languages. Thanks to the varying pressure of the forearm, it is possible to reproduce all the nuances of the spoken language—including slurred notes and onomatopoeias. There are, of course, a number of words with identical musicality and, in order to avoid confusion, a type of code has to be agreed upon between the player and his listeners. The language played on the hour-glass drum, however, is relatively straightforward in comparison with certain other forms of drummed message.

In fact, the hour-glass drum is unknown in many countries and another type of drum is used for the same purpose. It is made from a length of hollow tree trunk and has no skin. The tree trunk is carefully and skillfully hollowed out, leaving a cylinder with a longitudinal slit with two tongues, one male and one female.[84] The tongues are of unequal thickness so that they produce different notes. The average slit-drum is about 3 feet long, although it can range from a minimum of 1 foot, 6 inches to about 7 feet. The diameter is usually

A family of drums: father, mother, son, and daughter (Ghana)

The Musical Instruments

somewhere between 8 inches and 1 foot, 6 inches, but it can be as much as 3 feet. The slit-drum can produce only two notes or, very occasionally, three. For this reason, the messages are nearly always coded and consist of a series of metaphorical phrases that can be applied to various events of a similar nature. For example, the arrival of white men, policemen, or other strangers in the village is signaled by the set phrase, "They are here . . . they are here"; similarly, when the fishermen return with their catch, the news is invariably announced with the message, "The carp is here . . . the carp is here . . . It wants money . . . it wants money," and the prospective customers rush to the river bank where a canoe filled with dumb but greedy carp is waiting.

Some slit-drums are given proper names, usually consisting of a proverb, symbol, or riddle: "Pain doesn't kill," "Death has no master," "The river always flows in its bed," "You can't fight a war with one arm," "Birds don't steal from empty fields," "Do you know what goes 'thwack'?" (answer: "A whip on the backside"). The real purpose of these names is not just to identify the instrument, but also to confer upon it the virtues that they describe or to remind the musician and his neighbours of the truths and moral precepts on which everyday actions should be based. Occasionally, the name is a reminder of the circumstances under which the drum is to be played; the drum which announces happy events is not used to spread news of deaths and "Dancers, get in line" would be the name of an instrument used to introduce dances.

Slit-drum with carved ends (Cameroon)

A wrestling match in Ziguinchor (Senegal)

Although the slit-drum is best known to Africanists as a means of tele-graphy, it is also used as a musical instrument to accompany dancing. Hence, the following riddle that covers both these aspects: "I've got a dead prisoner at home, but when I want him to he can talk to people all over the country, or sing to encourage them to dance. Who is he?"

Bantu wrestling matches are always preceded by dancing. Two opposing teams are about to meet. Before they take their place in the crowded village square, the respective champions dance to the rhythm of the slit-drums, which simultaneously sing the praises of the dancers: "Champion, have you ever met your match? Who can rival you, tell us who? These poor creatures from Bassem think they can beat you with some poor devil they call a champion . . . but no one could ever beat you . . ." This is played by the drum of one team. The musicians belonging to the rival camp hear and understand these insults and their own drum quickly finds a reply: "The little monkey . . . the little monkey . . . he wants to climb the tree but everyone thinks he'll fall. But the little monkey is stubborn, he won't fall off the tree, he'll climb right to the top, this little monkey.'' And the drums will go on enlivening the proceedings throughout the entire wrestling match.

When the festivities are over, slit-drums and drums with skins are put away in special places prepared for that purpose (drum huts, the *Senufo* sacred wood, etc.); these places are not accessible to all. There is an atmosphere of magic in these places and the drums are revered as supernatural creatures. Some instruments are only removed from their hiding places very briefly on rare occasions. The *Kuyu* of Congo-Brazzaville bring out the seven sacred drums of the *Ikuma* sect exclusively for burials. They are played from the moment that they emerge until they go back into hiding after they have accompanied the incantations at the burial place.[85] When this short period is over, they retreat into their customary silence. In the *Dogon* territory of Mali, drums play an equally functional music during the dance of the *Kanagas*. In this dance, huge cross-shaped masks that represent the crocodile on whose back the ancestors of the *Dogon* crossed the River Niger to settle on the cliffs of Bandiagara (where their descendants live to this very day) are used.[86]

It would be impossible in such a brief study to enumerate all of the occasions when drums are used and the roles that they fulfil or even to attempt to describe them all; justice could not be done to their astonishing variety in a rapid inventory. Therefore, we shall make a limited selection based on the best available recordings of drum music that will give a faithful picture of one of the most characteristic aspects of African life.

Hour-glass and slit-drums with their variety of sounds are, as we have just seen, commonly used to transmit messages. But whereas the range of hour-glass drums is theoretically infinite due to the pressure exerted on the thongs, the slit-drum is restricted to two or three notes. As though to compensate for this, the *Malinke* musicians of Guinea, Mali, and parts of Senegal have invented an instrument known as the xylophone-drum, which has more than three notes. The xylophone-drum consists of a fairly long piece of hollow wood with longitudinal grooves of unequal length. Each pair of grooves forms a key and each key emits a different note when struck. It is, in other words, a tubular wooden drum with no membrane.

Single-headed drums are also used to send messages in many parts of West Africa. They are a means of communication whose symbolism has not been wasted on certain radio stations. ''Progress in the service of tradition'' could be the motto of Radio Ghana, for instance, which has for years been announcing its news broadcasts with a recording of these drums . . . ''speaking'' English! The signature tune that invites listeners to lend an ear to the news bulletins is played by two drums, with the words, ''Ghana, listen . . . Ghana, listen'' (C_2 G_2 C_2 C_2 . . . C_2 G_2 C_2 C_2).

Although the principal function of these drums is telegraphy, they are also formed into orchestras. They invariably retain their individual characteristics, however, and produce music in which the rhythm and tone of speech predominate. They are usually six in number, rather like a family consisting of a father,

Dogon drum and Kanaga *mask (Mali)*

mother, and four children. The *Grinpri Senufo* percussion band that has been
recorded in the Ivory Coast is of this type.[87] The central drum is so large that it
has to be held at an angle and supported by a stake that is planted in the ground.
It has a single head and is played with wooden sticks. This big drum is played
only in honour of the chief or other important personalities. "The ritual
salutations it raps out dominate the other drums." Meanwhile, three smaller,
one-headed drums play steady rhythmic patterns, reinforced by the chiming of
an iron bell. Finally, two one-headed drums that are tuned to two principal

speech tones and are played by a single musician armed with two hammer-like sticks, contribute to the liveliness of the group with their rhythmical phrases. The recording of *Yoruba* drums played by a group of professional musicians is somewhat similar. This *griot* orchestra comes from the Oyon region of western Nigeria; this region and Dahomey form the home of the *Yoruba*. Mr. Gilbert Rouget presents the orchestra in these words:[88] "The type of drum ensemble heard here should ideally consist of six drums and two is the bare minimum. The smallest drum provides a continuous rhythmic pulsation to support the second drum (*iya ilu*: mother drum) which plays a series of rhythmic phrases of varying length that are modified and combined in a multitude of ways, the whole based on the drum language technique known throughout Africa." Another example is the recording of a *Ba-Kongo-Nseke* drum ensemble[89] who perform a piece of music that is sometimes heard at the end of a period of mourning. The leading drum (the mother) of this ensemble is almost cylindrical and the center of its membrane is covered with resinous paste. The amount of paste regulates the pitch of the drum. The noise of the spherical rattles that the musician wears on each wrist contributes its part to the music. In addition to the "mother" drum, there are two other cylindrical, single-headed drums (without the addition of resin) and all three are beaten with the bare hands.

The West African talking drum is by no means the only drum used in percussion bands or instrumental ensembles. A rather unusual drum that is known as the friction-drum can be heard in a *Ba Lari* (Congo) orchestra;[90] it is a cylindrical drum with one-nailed head. A wooden stick that is hidden inside the cylinder is attached firmly to the center of the membrane. The stick is moved about so that it rubs against the membrane and causes it to vibrate. Before taking the stick in his right hand, the musician dampens it with a drop of water. As he plays, he exerts pressure on the drum-head with his left hand in order to modify the tension and vary the pitch of the sounds produced. The result is rather unexpected and sometimes gives the impression that an animal is talking, singing, or roaring rhythmically in the midst of the orchestra.

The friction-drum is, in fact, used in some parts of Africa to imitate the panther. An illustration of this, recorded in the Ivory Coast, is the music that is played during the visit of that inseparable couple Pondo Kaku and Goli who are together the most powerful of the genii who watch over the village.[91] The *Baule* call upon Pondo Kaku and Goli in times of epidemic or to punish adulterous wives—"They are the policemen of morals and mete out punishment to the guilty. Apart from these special occasions when they are summoned to the village, they pay regular visits and at each new moon they make the rounds of the village chasing away evil spirits." It was during one of the latter visits that Goli spoke with his "panther voice"—the panther being a dangerous animal symbolizing strength and intelligence.

Another variety of drum that is worthy of mention is the water-drum (*Gi dunu*) of the *Malinke* (Guinea, Mali, and Senegal); it is also found among the *Senufo* (Ivory Coast, Upper Volta, and Mali). The *Gi dunu* consists of two

Two drums—two notes that set the feet dancing or speak: "Ghana, listen . . . Ghana, listen . .

large hemispheric calabashes that are filled with water. They are placed side by side and two smaller, upturned half-calabashes float on the water. They are played with a type of stick or mallet that is made from a small calabash spoon; one is used in each hand. The level of the water in each drum is regulated in advance so that each of the upturned, floating recipients produces a different note when struck. Such drums provide a very pleasant sound and, particularly among the *Senufo*, are often played by women. Several recordings are available.[92]

Most *Senufo* villages are built near a ''sacred wood'' where the *poro*, a male secret society, carries out its initiation rites. Masks and certain musical instruments are also kept in the sacred wood and are only brought out when they are needed for a particular rite. These musical instruments, especially the drums, are normally played by men only, as is the case in most African societies. The ''Women's Drum''[93] that was recorded in *Senufo* country is, therefore, of singular interest; this is particularly true because the instrument is not, as might be expected, the *Gi dunu* water-drum. These women are actually playing a type of drum that is normally reserved for male use. However, not just any *Senufo* woman is allowed to play these four-footed drums that belong to the female *poro* society; this right is reserved exclusively for members of the *Fodonon* tribe.

We shall not at this point go into further detail about the role of the drum in initiation ceremonies; the reader may wish to turn back to page 10 where the *Lohu* ceremony of the *Adiukru* (Ivory Coast) is described at length.

Drums, which are virtually a male prerogative, also pervade the spiritual and mystical aspects of African life. The *Bata* drums that are used by the *Yoruba* of Dahomey to salute their divinities are but one example. There are some magnificent recordings of these *Bata* drums[94] that are at times played in pairs. ''The smaller one plays a fixed tattoo. The larger one salutes the divinities (*Orisha*) in the *Nago* tongue. The drum is spindle-shaped and the larger of the two skins is spread with a resinous paste. This paste allows the drum to be tuned. A little bell inside the drum jingles to the rhythm of the drum beats.''

The *Ba-benzele* Pygmies have a set of drums made along similar lines that they use to accompany the ritual music that is played on the eve of a hunting expedition. There are three single-headed drums: the male (*Motopai*), the female (*Maitu*), and the child (*Mona*). The wooden trunk is shaped like a tall mortar. The antelope-hide skin that covers the widest part of the barrel is tied to the drum with lianas and the tension of the skin is assured by a number of large wooden wedges. The female drum is smaller than the male drum, but is identical in shape. The drums are laid on the ground, parallel to one another, and the musicians straddle them and beat the skins with their hands. They can muffle or vary the pitch of certain notes by pressing the skin with one heel.[95]

African court music is by no means backward in employing percussion instruments, in general, and drums, in particular. Several recordings exist of an

That inseparable pair Pondo Kaku and Goli—the most powerful of the genii who protect Baule villages (Ivory Coast)

imposing Rwandese percussion band—the seven royal drums that once symbolized the sovereign power of the *mwami* (king). The royal family of Rwanda who came from the *Tutsi* tribe (about 17 percent of the total population) has recently been overthrown by the *Hutus* (who represent over 80 percent of the population). Thus, the documents collected in 1954–1955 (that is, before the fall of the monarchy) "as part of the research carried out by the Institute for Scientific Research in Central Africa in Rwanda-Burundi" now have a historical value.[96] In this recording, the seven royal drums were played by the musicians who had the exclusive right to play them. The privilege of playing the royal drums was reserved for the aristocracy and was handed down from father to son. While the musicians themselves—some ten in number—played in unison, the large drums that produce a muted sound were held in equilibrium by men of lowly social condition who crouched in front of the musicians. The ensemble is rather monotonous which is perhaps indicative of the complacency of the monarchy itself. The voice of a singer who extolls the king adds a more interesting note, but unfortunately, the recording does not do this nuance justice.

Court music is not restricted to praises or entertainments, but is used to accompany the daily activities of the monarch. The recording of the "Band of Six Drums"[97] that is used to wake the *mwami* is an example of this fact. The six drums that are used are all played by the same person, accompanied by another musician singing the praises of the six sacred drums or royal emblems.

Other interesting specimens of the role of drums in court music were recorded among the *Mossi* of Upper Volta: "The traditional orchestra of the *Naba* of Tenkodogo" and "A drum reciting the genealogy of the *Naba*."[98] A *Naba* is a traditional *Mossi* chief. The *Mossi*, who are the largest ethnic group in Upper Volta, probably originated in the South. "They installed their first Kingdom in Tenkodogo before heading north as far as Ouagadougou and Ouahigouya. There is still a traditional chief, or *Moro Naba*, in each of these three towns (the senior of the three being the *Moro Naba* of Ouagadougou who succeeded Naba Oubri, the founder of the dynasty)."[99]

The recordings that are mentioned above were made at the court of Naba Tigre, the *Naba* of Tenkodogo. "This is the traditional orchestra attached to his person and consists of twelve drums: Six large calabashes (*Binha*), four double-headed drums (*Gangado*) and two hour-glass drums (*Luinsse*). The orchestra accompanies the voice of Tala Kere, a *griot* who majestically declaims the history of the nabas of Tenkodogo. This is an amazing historical document which has been faithfully transmitted from generation to generation without the aid of writing! The drums of Naba Tigre's orchestra actually do the talking, the singer merely translates, or to be more accurate, transposes. This is particularly evident in the second recording, in which the soloist Bend Naba makes his drum "talk" while Bila Balima uses his voice to transpose."[100]

Bamun music is very diversified and also furnishes some fascinating examples of court music. "Where do the *Bamun* come from, these tall, stout

Ba-Lari *woman playing a friction-drum (Congo)*

warriors and farmers, with their large, almost semitic noses, light skins and
ample gestures, that give the women in particular a certain elegance which
recalls Juno rather than Aphrodite? According to tradition their birthplace was
the village of Rifoum in the plains north-east of the grassy plateaux where they
now dwell, in the extreme west of Cameroon . . .'' They have intermixed with
various neighbouring tribes (the *Tikar, Mbum,* and *Bamileke*) and their country
has throughout history been a real ''crossroads of races and civilizations,''
especially since ''the beginning of the 19th century when the *Fulbe* shepherds,
led by the prophet Ousman Dan Fodio, first made their appearance in the
Bamun plateaux.'' Nevertheless, the *Bamun* have managed to keep their

Two water-drums

These Tuareg women (Niger) provide their own rhythmic accompaniment by drumming and clapping their hands.

Bamun *"Music for the Hanging of a Minister"* (Cameroon)

These snare drums bridge the generation gap with their music.

This long drum is attached to a pole that holds it in position.

Togolese drums

The Musical Instruments

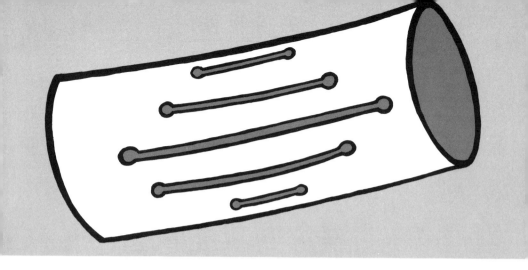

Xylophone-drum

Double metal bell

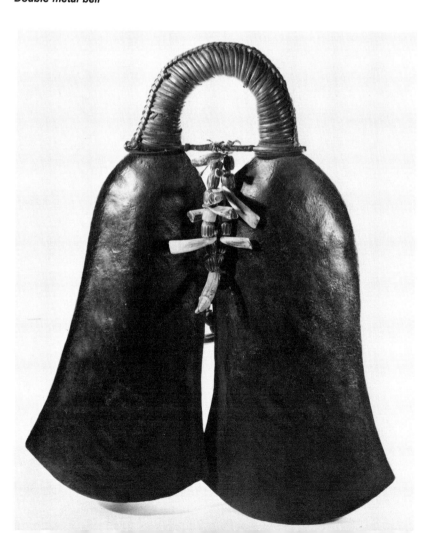

The drum orchestra of the Naba (traditional chief) of Tenkodogo (Upper Volta)

individuality, "thanks to a political structure totally centred around the king and his palace, a vast enclosure which is still the centre of the *Bamun* capital, Foumban. The king is an absolute monarch who is law-giver, judge, general and patron. *Bamun* art is subject to royal command."

"*Bamun* art is not therefore popular art but court art. *Bamun* music is also an inter-tribal art, which combines the diverse influences which have penetrated the country. This diversity of origin results in a vast range of musical instruments, which are however used with discretion."

This quotation is taken from Louis C. D. Joos's introduction to a recording of "*Bamun* Dances and Songs," made in the palace of the Sultan of Foumban and in the presence of the reigning Sultan, Seidou Njoya Njimouluh.

Among the items on this record is the extraordinary "Music for the Hanging of a Minister"[101] which, despite the presence of five percussion instruments (three iron bells and two drums), has a sobriety that enhances the lugubrious nature of the occasion. The rhythm hardly varies throughout the entire proceedings and inexorably underlines the ultimate sentence that was passed on the king's minister who was found guilty of a serious crime—a crime punishable only by death. To the sound of the imperturbable and menacing percussion, a herald in a voice filled with emotion translates the meaning of the music:

> This music is never heard without grave cause.
> Whoever hears it will anxiously wonder:
> "Is it for me, is it for my neighbour?"
> There lies the danger.
> A chasm in front, a chasm behind.
> This music has no friend.
> It is good only when it recedes
> And fatal when it approaches.

We shall not claim to have said all that there is to say about African drums. We have by no means exhausted a subject which, as already mentioned, is far too vast for a study of this size. We hope, however, that these few pages that are based upon recordings that are worthy of notice have given the reader some useful examples of the use of the African drum. It goes without saying that these are not the only recordings available. The drum is, moreover, the most representative and best-known percussion instrument and automatically covers the whole field of African music. Records of traditional music that are without at least one example of percussion are rare, as the admirable "Anthology of the Music of Chad"[102] demonstrates.

Beside drums, there are, of course, a number of other percussion instruments such as bells or gourds.[103] And some African musicians even manage to obtain percussion effects with melodic instruments. Some of the one-stringed lute or harp-lute (*Kora, Seron*) solos that are mentioned in the section on stringed instruments bear witness to this. The tendency to generalize "drumming" exists in other forms of Negro music as well. Negro-American bass players in the 1930s used to pluck the strings of their instruments so that the notes were accompanied by the rhythm of the strings as they struck the bridge.

Even the human voice is not exempt from the insatiable desire to drum. Some African singers achieve a vibrato effect by moving their tongue rapidly from one side of their mouth to the other, so that their tongue strikes the inside of their cheeks. Some African languages are naturally percussive; this is particularly true of the *Bantus* of South Africa: Miriam Makeba uses these "clicks" in the traditional *Zulu* songs that form part of her repertoire.

Many African griots stop their ears with their hands when they sing.

African Music

THE HUMAN VOICE

We shall conclude with a few remarks about the human voice—the musical instrument most widely used by Africans, as an examination of available records will demonstrate. Even if we were to put all the recordings where the voice is of secondary importance into the instrumental category, we would still be left with a ratio of about two vocals to every instrumental piece. Vocal music is truly the essence of African musical art. This fact in no way diminishes the interest of musical instruments; on the contrary, since the prime motive of the instruments is to reconstitute spoken or sung language, they have a significance which is unparalleled in the music of other continents.

The utilization of the voice by musicians in black Africa—its timbres and the different nuances obtained by means of artifices unknown to the rest of the world (stopping the ears, pinching the nose, vibrating the tongue in the mouth, producing echoes by directing the voice into a receptacle, etc.)—largely accounts for the confusion, or rather, the incomprehension that almost inevitably confronts the non-African listener when he at first hears black African music.

Before we go any further, we must emphasize that the notion of a "beautiful singing voice"—one of the most subjective notions imaginable—cannot be applied to the letter as far as black singers are concerned. A Negro musician may happen to have a beautiful voice by Western standards, but this does not mean that his music springs from Western criteria—criteria such as melodic perfection, correctness of pitch, finish, or purity of tone. A beautiful voice (again in the Western sense) may be a mere accident in the context of traditional African music. The objective of African music is not necessarily to produce sounds agreeable to the ear, but to translate everyday experiences into living sound. In a musical environment whose constant purpose is to depict life, nature, or the supernatural, the musician wisely avoids using beauty as his criterion because no criterion could be more arbitrary.

Consequently, African voices adapt themselves to their musical context—a mellow tone to welcome a new bride; a husky voice to recount an indiscreet adventure; a satirical inflection for a teasing tone, with laughter bubbling up to compensate for the mockery—they may be soft or harsh as circumstances demand. Any individual who has the urge to make his voice heard is given the liberty to do so; singing is not a specialized affair. Anyone can sing and, in practice, everyone does.

This is the essence of the collective aspect of African music; no one is ruled out because he is technically below par. Vocal music is vitally important in this respect because it gives the people who perform it every day of their lives a confirmation of the social significance of their art. Therefore, it is hardly necessary to add that it is vocal music alone that can adequately express the meaning of a rite, offer up a prayer to the gods, pronounce sentence and order execution, or preach love and unity within the community.

But when we come to the specialists—the aforementioned *griots* and "zither-touchers"—song becomes an art. It is this art, usually patiently studied under the guidance of a teacher, that gives these castes of troubadours, who have since time immemorial been the custodians of tradition, their principal *raison d'être*. A *griot* who could not sing would be a contradiction in terms. Yet the art of singing remains purely functional and could not be labelled academic or esoteric. It retains a simplicity of form that makes it readily accessible to all, so that a *griot* may be no more than the soloist in a group of singers, a conductor among musicians who, without necessarily being specialists, still know the score at least in its broad outline.

A characteristic of all African music is the fact that it is common property—a language that all members of any one ethnic group can understand. Whereas in the instrumental field, there are a few learned forms and techniques that are beyond the possibilities of all but a handful of initiates, vocal music is truly popular. It draws its inspiration from the people and graciously endows the most banal event with philosophic wisdom.

For all of these reasons, African vocal music is a worthwhile topic of investigation for anyone who is not only interested in the ups and downs of daily life to which it relates, but who is even interested in certain aspects of African philosophy.

It may seem paradoxical to devote so little space to the human voice after having emphasized its overriding importance as compared with musical instruments. But then again, there is such a variety of African vocal music on records that it seemed unfair to single out just a few illustrations. The sleeve-notes of the records frequently explain the meaning of the lyrics and sometimes give a full translation.[104] In any event, the number of songs that are totally lacking in interest is minimal, as the commentaries and explanations given on the record sleeves will corroborate.

This brief review of musical instruments has given us the opportunity to dismiss one or two myths, in particular the well-known cliché that traditional African music is represented exclusively by the drum. As we have pointed out, black Africa can boast an impressive number of musical instruments of all kinds. Each one has its own irreplaceable attributes and role and to overlook any of them or relegate them to a secondary rank would arise from sheer ignorance. And, although this music has a very special role—because it is often linked to rites that are exclusive to the African continent—the instruments themselves, both in conception and category, are proof that African music is not so unlike music in any other part of the world.

We are certain that the reader of this text will discover by listening to some of the records that we have recommended throughout these pages that this music, which may seem so different from his own, is not nearly as unprepossessing as it may at first appear.

If an objective approach of this kind leads the reader to become a real devotee of African music, the author of these lines will be more than gratified.

"I came to play my drum for the dancing, not to deliver a slave into bondage."

The Musical Instruments

This harp, which is often used by man to communicate with the other world, shows the close link between sculpture and music.

The Music

WHICH CAME FIRST, speech or song? In the case of Africa it is virtually impossible to estimate. On the other hand, it is a fact that much African music is based on speech. The bond between language and music is so intimate that it is actually possible to tune an instrument so that the music it produces is linguistically comprehensible. The language "spoken" by the slit-drum, for instance, is so realistic and specific that the messages it transmits can only be understood by members of the community where that particular language is spoken.

We can illustrate this fact by relating a true story about a European girl in Africa who bought a *mvet*. She took it to show her father's chauffeur who, so it was said, could play this kind of instrument. The African examined the harp-zither very carefully for a few moments and tentatively plucked the strings. Then, he handed it back to her in apparent disgust, explaining that he had no way of communicating with "someone who did not speak the same language" as he did. Not surprisingly, the girl, because she was no ethnomusicologist, was more than puzzled by this talk of communication with an instrument—an instrument that the chauffeur called a "man." If she had been acquainted with any authentic, traditional African musicians, she would have realized that a musical instrument "speaks" the same language as does its player and that it is often regarded as a human being. Playing a musical instrument is virtually a form of communication, not to say communion, between the musician and his instrument. Obviously, music in black Africa has a much wider significance, even on a personal level, than is at first realized.

This story reminds us of a personal experience that took place in Upper Volta where we were presenting a live-radio broadcast in Ouagadougou. The programme included traditional dances that were performed by groups from various parts of the country. The instruments of one of these groups included a remarkable set of six drums that were made from dried and hollowed calabashes which had been covered with skins. They are called *Bendere* and Upper Volta seems to be the only country in Africa where such drums exist. Apart from their rarity, they are also extremely beautiful instruments and, not unnaturally, we were rather eager to obtain one. Our attempts to persuade one of the musicians to sell his drum were fruitless; the increasingly tempting sums that we offered were systematically refused. Despite his evident poverty, he could not bear the idea of parting with the instrument. We finally admitted defeat and asked him why he had so categorically refused. He replied rather dryly that he had come to town to play his drum for the dancing and not to deliver a slave into bondage. He too looked upon his instrument as a person, a colleague who spoke the same language and helped him to create his music. The instrument itself, as a mere object, is not important; what matters is the music that is produced and the vital relationship that exists between the instrument and the player as joint creators. Musical instruments are symbols of the Creation—a time when God imbued man with life and speech.

Music thus grows out of the intonations and rhythmic onomatopoeias of speech. In song these intonations must be respected. In the *Duala* language, which is typical of *Bantu* languages, any melodic contradiction betwen the way a word is spoken and the way it is sung is inconceivable. For example, the noun *moto* (which means "man," as opposed to an animal) is said on one note with identical stress on both syllables; this accentuation is adhered to in all *Duala* songs; if the two syllables were sung on different notes, the word would lose its meaning. *Muto* ("woman"), on the other hand, is said on two different notes. The first is higher than the second (that is, if *mu* were an A_3 *to* would be an F_3). The pitch of these sounds is respected in all traditional *Duala* vocal music and no one would dream of inversing it; the composition of the song is patterned on the music of the spoken word.

Thus it is quite a simple matter to glide progressively from speech into song as the *mvet* harp-zither players do in their narratives. The pastors of the black religious communities that are many thousands of miles away in the United States have the same facility. The American Negro has managed by trial and error to transform the white man's language into a singing language whose intonations resemble his ancestral tongues. The shifting of the tonic accent, the ellipse of certain syllables, and the addition of percussive onomatopoeias, not to mention difficulties encountered in pronouncing some words correctly, have given us the jazz idiom, as well as the declamatory preaching style epitomized by the Rev. Kelsey. Despite obvious differences in musical style and context, the Rev. Kelsey and his congregation who were recorded in a black chapel in the United States still have a great deal in common with their brothers who remain in Africa.

The intonations of African languages represent much more than the tonic accents of Indo-European languages. A tonic accent is the stress placed on a particular syllable in a word, for example, the syllable "te" of the English word "material" or the syllable *nai* of the French word *dictionnaire*. African languages, and particularly *Bantu* languages, which are even more musical than the rest, contain something far more subtle—something that consists of a series of tied notes that cover intervals of one to three degrees. These degrees go from one syllable to the next. The note of the first syllable is not stressed more

As soon as the sound of these drums and the alghaita is heard in the village square, a crowd of admirers gathers around the musicians.

than that of the second; it is the music that unites the two syllables that gives the word its meaning. The musicality of many *Bantu* words is so precise that they can be transcribed on a stave, using European notation, for example *jiba* (theft in *Duala*) would be written:

while *muenen* (light) could be transcribed as:

We have dwelt on the importance of *language* in African music because this is what chiefly distinguishes it from the other art forms of black Africa. No other art is quite so specifically African. Any talented sculptor could reproduce a Negro mask or statuette, but music is quite another matter; it entails the use of instruments that are made specifically in order to express a chosen language in musical terms. It is scarcely an exaggeration to say that without African languages, African music would not exist. Authentic African music presupposes a practical knowledge of any one African language. English and French have been adopted as official languages in most modern African states, but although they may eventually replace African languages in many walks of life, they will never be able to do so in music—unless a deliberate decision is taken to deform the art of traditional music. The tendency to neglect the study of vernacular languages is another of the crises facing the African musician.

Western distinctions between instrumental and vocal music are evidently unthinkable in Africa where the human voice and musical instruments "speak" the same language, express the same feelings, and unanimously recreate the universe each time that thought is transformed into sound. Consequently, the words with which they acclaim life are articulated in an equally careful manner. This connection between music and words has not escaped the attention of all Europeans. The producers of a record entitled "A Panorama of the Instrumental Music of Black Africa"[1] found the task of recording only instruments impossible and were obliged, therefore, to include a number of recordings in which the human voice is by no means relegated to the background.

The above discussion might give the impression that a knowledge of one or more of the African languages is a prerequisite to the enjoyment of African music. If this were the case, African music would find itself in a linguistic ghetto—a situation that would preclude any form of expansion. Fortunately, this is not the case. Music is primarily a matter of sounds that have an intrinsic value that transcends linguistic barriers. It is a music that appeals directly to the

What is music? It is the total expression of life, shared by all the senses.

The Music

ear. A true understanding of African music does, as we have already pointed out, demand patience and objectivity. The development of this understanding applies not only to non-Africans, but also to Africans who must make a similar effort to understand the music of societies other than their own. Seen in this light, the art of African music reveals so many different facets that it may be justifiable to speak of the various kinds of African music, rather than merely using the global expression, "African music." There is, however, a certain unity in all of the music that encourages us to speak of "African music," regarding it as a kaleidoscope of different sounds that are in harmony with various languages and dialects.

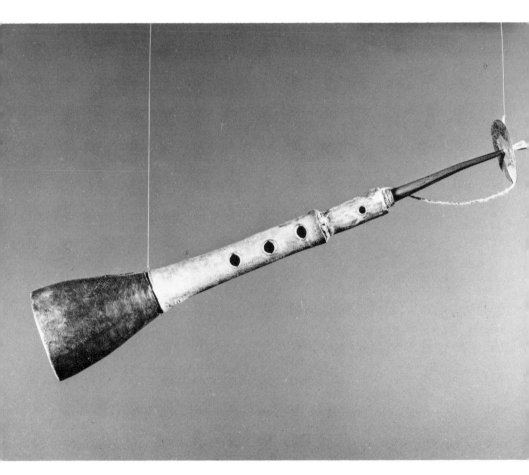

The alghaita is one of the rare instruments that sings its music rather than speaking it.

Many of the characteristics that give African music its unity have already been discussed in previous chapters and thus, they can be summarized briefly as follows: The manufacture, tone, and function of the instruments that are found in various parts of Africa are more or less consistent; music is often collective, even communal, and plays a social, therapeutic, or magic role in society. However, before we mention various other general characteristics, we must emphasize that it would be wrong to imagine that all African music necessarily has a particular role or function. A nightwatchman who plays his *Sanza* and sings of his hopes or misfortunes does not concern himself with the social role of his music; he is playing in order to pass the time. This being said, let us return

Almost every sound of nature can be reproduced with the aid of ingenious instruments such as this rattle, consisting of a calabash and some millet stalks.

The Music

to our main subject—the music played in most of the villages of the African continent.

The first thing that attracts attention is its vitality. Music is a challenge to human destiny; a refusal to accept the transience of this life; and an attempt to transform the finality of death into another kind of living. This eruption of life tends to bewilder the non-African in his initial contact with the black musical world. He is often startled to discover that funeral music in African societies can be as gay and tumultuous as a marriage feast. This shock occurs because he is accustomed to mourn his dead in reverential silence. The traditions of one world may be profoundly shocking to those who were raised to accept other convictions. But mourning in African society is both a physical and an emotional act and the sound of trumpets or drums in no way diminishes for the African the sincerity of the tears he sheds for the dead. Moreover, the concept of life and death transcends physical notions of noise or silence. It has a metaphysical dimension that is reflected in these words of a black poet, speaking on behalf of his people:

> Those who are dead are never gone:
> They are in the brightening Shadow
> And in the thickening Gloom.
> The Dead are not beneath the Earth:
> They are in the quivering Tree,
> They are in the groaning Wood,
> They are in the flowing Water,
> And in the still Water,
> They are in the Hut, they are in the Crowd:
> The Dead are not dead.[2]

This conviction as expressed by the poet softens the tragic moments of transition from life to afterlife. In other parts of the world, such grief would be translated into the minor mode. The African, however, confronts death with the rhythms and music of life. His attitude reveals perhaps the true meaning of life, music, and man himself. But it is the crux of the incomprehension that exists between the musician and the nonmusician; however, according to Mr. Charles Duvelle all art is based on some degree of incomprehension.[3]

This brings us to the threshold of a long discussion that will, if it is fruitful, lead to the progressive appreciation of values, which we said at the outset were supposedly misunderstood by non-Africans. It will, however, be pointless if it falls on closed minds or on the minds of those who refuse to make any positive concessions concerning black African music. This is a question that concerns not just African music, but music in general, or any art form. African music may be approached as any other art form that is at first new or strange. Most of us experience a certain bewilderment, sometimes a positive uneasiness, the first time that we step into the world of creations by Picasso or Braque, Calder or Giacometti, Brancusi or Moore. If we eventually grow to admire and then love

Rhythm is the reflection of the constant presence of music.

The Music

the worlds of these artists, it is because we are attracted and held by the life that they reveal.

This growing sense of appreciation can be equally applied to the art of African music. An objective approach will be well-rewarded and will reveal a fascinating new world—not merely the expression of one isolated individual, but that of an entire, vast continent. This continent at its present state of evolution still possesses a "power of persuasion and a spirit of unanimity which speaks to and for the collectivity."[4]

Another feature that is common to all types of music in black Africa is rhythm. It is easy to recognize but hard to define. Some people regard it as a purely mechanical thing—the periodic repetition of downbeats and upbeats that mark given musical phrases. Others believe it is a kind of magic that is exclusive to Negroes who employ it in order to render their music "bewitching" or "satanic." The truth lies somewhere between these two viewpoints. Rhythm is an invisible covering that envelops each note or melodic phrase that is destined to speak of the soul or to the soul; it is the reflection of the constant presence of music. It is the element that infuses music with a biological force that brings forth a psychological fruit. Rhythm is a support or catalyst and not a musical form in its own right. Furthermore, "it is no longer possible to uphold the theory that African music is essentially rhythmic and that melody is reduced to short, endlessly repeated phrases. It does in fact frequently contain a high degree of melodic development and the use of polyphony is more widespread in Africa than it is in Europe."[5]

Mr. Paul Collaer's remarks can easily be verified by listening to those recordings that present various pieces of African music in their entirety. Such recordings are relatively few in number, but "The Music of the Princes" (Dahomey),[6] "Pondo Kaku" (Ivory Coast), [7] and "Edzingi's Dance" provide convincing evidence of melodic development in African music. The music that accompanies "Edzingi's Dance" (recorded in 1946 by Mr. Gilbert Rouget of the Musée de l'Homme in Paris)[8] forms part of the hunting ritual of the *Babinga Bangombe* Pygmies. The full ceremony lasts for several hours and is usually repeated several days in succession. It would not, therefore, be feasible to issue a recording of the whole dance, but the extracts on the aforementioned record represent the most important episodes. Pygmies live by hunting, gathering wild fruits, and bartering with the "tall men" who dwell at the edge of the forest. The *Bangombe* inhabit the Ouessa Region of Congo (Brazzaville) on the left bank of the River Sangho, north of the confluent of the Ngoko.

"When the *Bangombe* have killed a male elephant with long tusks they call Edzingi, a monster who lives in the forest and invite him to come and dance. The role of Edzingi is played by a young man disguised in a voluminous raffia cloak—but no-one is supposed to realize this. He enters the camp, spinning like a top, dances, and then goes back into the forest to rest for a few moments before making another appearance. When he arrives the men shout shrill-voiced encouragements. Four drums beat unceasingly; one of the men

After a successful hunt, they dance for joy; before a hunt, they dance in hope. The life of the Pygmies is always set to music.

The Music

strikes a metal bell. The women, who are crowded together a little way off, sing and clap their hands. The men form a circle round Edzingi and crowd about him as they dance.

"The ceremony unfolds like a play. At the end Edzingi falls to the ground, picks himself up but falls again and lies motionless for several minutes. When he finally stands up he goes back into the forest and disappears. The music follows the various stages of the dance. . . .

"Both musically and choreographically the Edzingi ceremony must be considered as an ensemble of movements which develops along certain lines and forms a whole. . . .

"The first movement—waiting for the arrival of Edzingi, who is still in the forest—typifies the opening of the ceremony and is characterized by the absence of drums, the importance of the solo voice and a fairly simple choral division.

"The second extract represents a particularly intense episode in 'Edzingi's Dance' and is characterized by the fullness and complexity of the polyphony, the variety of means successively employed and the occurrence of cries (hunting calls), which all contribute to the excitement.

"Polyphonic shouting, in which women's voices predominate, is one of the most original traits of Pygmy vocal technique. Alternation between polyphonic shouting and polyphonic singing is a characteristic feature of *Babinga* musical composition and the transition from one to the other takes place without interruption. Pygmy dance music is formed of a series of relatively short movements (2 to 3 minutes) with interruptions whose length depends on the circumstances and type of dance. Edzingi is no exception to either of these rules.

"The end of the ceremony—what we might call the death agony of Edzingi—is marked by an entirely new musical theme which, as the dance proceeds, undergoes a gradual, imperceptible transformation until finally, when Edzingi disappears, it has become a psalmody of a completely different nature to everything that has preceded. The piece ends with the shouts which accompany Edzingi as he returns to the forest."[9]

The Pygmies are believed to be the earliest inhabitants of Africa and their music is in every sense authentically African. It is totally collective, not at all monotonous, deeply significant, and indisputably it plays an integral part in black African life. Many features of Pygmy music are shared by the music of other peoples: the importance of the human voice, polyphony, shouting, songs that are accompanied by hand-clapping, developments or changes in musical themes to fit various episodes of the choreography (for choreography, read "life"), and so on.

But although African music contains many universal elements such as these, it is perhaps true that African musicians utilize them in what Westerners would consider an unorthodox manner. Before passing judgment, it would be as well to recall that Africans are not ignorant of Western techniques and

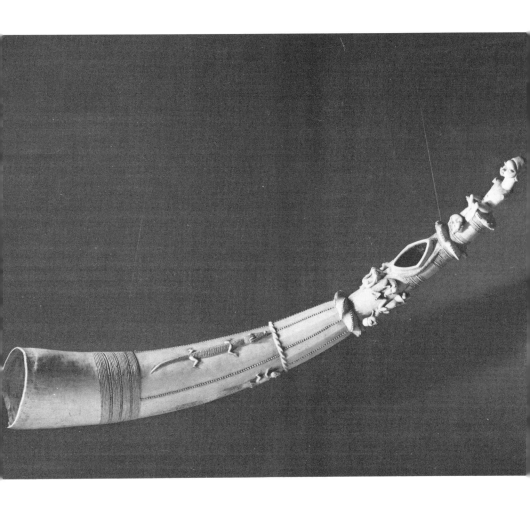

This legendary horn is the homonym of the one in the Roncevaux epic—a bond between two worlds and two cultures.

The Music

principles; they merely see them from a different point of view.

It is said that black voices are not trained. They are, in fact, but in a different way than non-African voices and for a different purpose. African singers have no need to use techniques to develop tessitura or to obtain the vocal pitch and accuracy that are required for the opera stage or the concert platform. Rather, their task is to speak the everyday language that the average person can understand; why, then, should they spend hours practicing scales? African voices are used to echo the speech and thoughts of the people as faithfully as possible and without embellishment. Their technique is a quest for truth. An African singer will stutter if he is singing about a stammerer or will literally attempt to tie his tongue in knots when he has something difficult to say. He cups his hands over his ears to discover unusual sonorities and reproduces them with a dexterity that amazes and delights his listeners. The African singer alternates head and chest and voice like a game of hide-and-seek in a labyrinth of rhythm. Every note that he sings is a reflection of life itself and his technique is amply suited to this role of depicting life. His voice recreates a world of laughter and pain, mockery and praise; and it throws open the gates of time to reveal a glimpse of the future.

In other words, however transcendent the substance of African music may be, it is always expressed at a human level. This is perhaps the most baffling paradox of all; the celestial music that is raised to the glory of the gods has its roots in the terrestrial realities of daily life. (The arts of painting and sculpture in black Africa are, in this respect, comparable to music.)

If we examine this paradox more closely, we shall see why technique is less highly prized by Africans than it is by those in the West. In Europe, for example, a technically perfect musician is almost automatically classed as an artist. Technique and art are, however, two entirely different things and although they frequently go hand in hand, they often have different objectives. The aim of art is to create beauty and pleasure; technique may help to achieve this aim, but it is usually not an end in itself. In the West, a high level of technical skill is considered essential to the creation of a work of art. Technique should be the handmaiden of art, but all too often works of art are judged by the degree of technique involved; a wrong note, a false step, or a careless brush-stroke are judged inadmissible.

The African musician, on the other hand, is primarily concerned with the *art* of playing an instrument and not with the technique. Technique is an intermediary stage and once he has mastered the rudiments of his instrument, he pays little attention to it. This relatively brief period of apprenticeship explains why the same kind of instrument may be played in a multitude of different ways; technique is very much a matter of individual taste.

The absence of technique—in the Western sense of the term—does not imply a corresponding absence of artistry. Art is a utility and, as we have already seen, music is a necessity—a vital function. Music is the outward and audible manifestation of inward biological functions; it is the support and

Notes pointing up to the sky, to the glory of gods and great men

The Music

realization of their metaphysical purpose. For example, music cannot bring about the actual birth of a child, but it can help the child to live. The words of a lullaby not only wish the child a long and happy life, but also glorify the supernatural beings whose invisible presence is necessary in order for the wish to be realized.

This utterly disproves Mr. Robert Gay's statement that "Negro music is essentially physical."[10] Many of the records mentioned in this book adequately demonstrate the spiritual qualities of African music.

Once we have grasped the importance that life holds for the African, his music becomes much easier to explain and understand. Birth and rebirth are the key words in the simplest of cycles. Music is born with each child and accompanies him throughout life. Music helps the child triumph in his first encounter with death—the symbolic death that precedes initiation; it is reborn with the child who is now a man and it directs his steps along the path of law and order that has been laid down by the community.

On that path, music and truth become one; order and rhythm become one. Musicality is no longer a mere word, but becomes a series of acts. Hence, the real disappointment of the foreigner arises when he vainly tries to grasp a melody, chord, or movement without seeing the music in its entirety. No matter, for African music goes blithely on its way with all of its vices and virtues and a total lack of concern for its own future. It is precisely this latter aspect of the African's philosophy that should merit our attention at the present time, a time when practical considerations are more urgent than musicological theories.

Many seminars and festivals have been organized during the past twenty years with the aim of bringing Negro arts—particularly African arts—to the attention of a wider public. By far the most important of these events was the First World Festival of Negro Arts which took place in Dakar in April of 1966. Parallel with the Festival, a Symposium on Negro Art was held under the auspices of Unesco and the African Cultural Society whose President is Mr. Alioune Diop, the Director of "Présence Africaine." This symposium gave Africanists from all over the world an opportunity to discuss many aspects of Negro art. Both present and future problems were examined by specialists who are fully aware of the potential role of Negro art in a world that is constantly in search of artistic renovation. The symposium was of capital importance because it defined the true place of African art and it also took a fresh look at its present and future role. The Cameroonian priest, Engelbert Mveng, wrote: "The message of such art can obviously never grow old. Consequently African art today must reflect the destiny of modern African man . . . But our chief desire is that, despite the vicissitudes of time, our artistic language will continue to be a form of humanism open to all humanity."[11]

It would, of course, be naïve to imagine that the major themes that were touched on in a meeting of this kind would instantly solve all the problems of

The quest for timbre in music can be compared with the quest for whatever is strange, extraordinary, or superhuman in sculpture or choreography.

African arts and artists, and the research into different spheres of this art are all still very much live issues. In fact, since the Festival revealed the artistic splendours of the past and enabled a comparison to be made with present-day production, these issues can now be seen within an even wider context.

This comparison between the past and present provoked a number of differing reactions. The most general of these was that as things stand at present, modern African art is qualitatively and quantitatively inferior to the art of earlier times. We are reluctant to concur with this judgment, particularly because the periods of time under consideration are very different. The exhibition of traditional African art that was held in Dakar in 1966—and which was subsequently shown in Paris the following summer—ranged from the fifteenth or sixteenth centuries up to the first few decades of the twentieth century. Under the circumstances, it is hardly surprising that the so-called ancient output proved to be quantitatively superior to what is classified as modern—a term that barely covers a period of thirty years.

As far as quality is concerned, we would be lacking in objectivity if we failed to recognize that in recent years African art has been in quest of its own identity. The enormous amount of foreign influence that has been infiltrating Africa since the beginning of the colonial era has in no way been counterbalanced by any sign of foreign encouragement for the indigenous arts. When, as so often happens, people ask us whether we think black African art can survive, we always feel tempted to reply, "African art is dead! Long live African art!"

This is not meant in jest, as a closer look at the context will reveal. Black Africa is evolving, birth and rebirth remain the eternal watchwords. The colonial period could be likened, on a much wider scale of course, to a period of initiation. A period of initiation is traditionally a time when future initiates leave their village and their old customs for several weeks and cloister themselves in the forest, in huts surrounded by high fences. During this retreat, they learn all that they need to know in order to take their rightful place in adult society. Sometimes, they are expected to give up certain of their former customs entirely, but often past experience and present reality are welded together into a new philosophy of life. The latter attitude is definitely more propitious to the flowering or expansion of new human qualities and a regenerated way of thinking.

We firmly believe that such welding and regeneration will be the pattern for African art. Many of the foreign influences that have penetrated Africa will be incorporated into a new form of black African art. This form of initiation may be deplored by those with deep-seated conservative or racialist tendencies, but far from resulting in a bastardized and damaging modernism, we believe this mutation will breathe new life into African art and will demonstrate the triumph of humanism and universality over esoteric sterility.

Most of the meetings that we have previously mentioned have resulted in recommendations having been made that concern the preservation and protec-

"Our chief desire is that, despite the vicissitudes of time, our art will continue to be a form of humanism open to all humanity."

tion of the arts. Recommendations have also been made concerning popularization; the implication is that African art will benefit from being better known by the general public. In our opinion, it is the public who will benefit from getting to know African art. However, these opinions are relative and depend on one's point of view. But, even if we restrict ourselves to the problems of the preservation and protection of African art, we still take a stand that some people may find disconcerting or even negative; in our view, in a century where survival depends upon development, the preservation of the arts has no urgent priority, unless such preservation is accompanied by developmental trends.

Particularly as far as music is concerned, the preservation of ancestral forms is meaningless unless it is part of a genuine development programme. We are, of course, delighted that the many excellent recordings that are now available permit people throughout the world to become acquainted with the purest form of African expression. We are also gratified to know that men of goodwill have gone to the trouble of recording African life in the belief that it is a new and interesting world—a world that is now preserved in European and American museums on miles of magnetic tape. This book would certainly never have been written if such efforts had not been made in recent years.

"African art is dead. Long live African art!"

But preservation just for the sake of preserving is one thing; it *merely* gives the satisfaction of knowing that every possible effort has been made to ensure that nothing in existence shall be lost. Selective preservation of what deserves to be kept is quite another matter. In the first instance, preservation will, in most cases, prove to be a waste of time. The second attitude is prompted by a dynamic and positive spirit of liberalism that turns its back on immobility and that is orientated toward development. And development is a form of preservation that keeps abreast of the times and, in the long run, gains time. We feel it is imperative that the future of African music be based on the idea of development and not merely upon preservation.

What form should this development take? Parallel with the efforts undertaken to collect, classify, and publish existing material, there is a need to establish centres for the development of African music. The "schools of art" that are springing up throughout Africa today should certainly not be suppressed, but special emphasis must be placed on the development of the *musical art*. Up until now, only a handful of specialists, mostly non-Africans, have taken a real interest in music. This fact is probably because music is more abstract than the plastic arts and also because it is associated with various other art forms and tends, therefore, to be overlooked.

Art is part and parcel of the corporate soul. All that can be captured on tape or record is a minute fraction of the emotions that are expressed by this soul and these media can never replace the soul itself—a soul that is the mother of expression. It is by no means a bad thing to preserve this fraction; on the contrary, it is useful to maintain a record of the different ways in which this expression manifests itself at different points in time. Pinpointing this expression at a given moment may be a useful contribution to the world of the arts. But it is by no means enough. People must be inspired with the urge to express themselves often, in an artistic language that takes account of their evolution. Sincere efforts of this kind have been made in a number of African countries during the past years. But they must be increased and coordinated if African music is to develop.

Among the practical ways in which this could be achieved, we would suggest the following objectives:

1. the organization of musical competitions and other cultural events that could be meeting places for traditional and modern musicians.
2. the creation of companies of folk artists to present genuine traditional art forms with special emphasis on music.
3. the formation of traditional orchestras that would receive financial assistance in order to enable them to remain in close contact with their ancestral art forms and to maintain a purity of expression.
4. the payment of all musicians who record for the radio or discs.
5. the promotion of traditional music by recording companies on a scale comparable with that used to sell pop songs.

6. the establishment of subsidized ethnomusicological research centres, African instrument-making centres, and conservatories of African music.

7. the broadcasting by African radio stations of as much African music as possible, with explanations and commentaries, so that Africans all over the continent could familiarize themselves with one another's music.

In this connection, it must be remembered that urban life, which exposes the African to European music, and the ever-growing exodus from villages to towns, have created a new breed of African—one who tends to resolutely turn his back on the traditional past. He may do this for reasons of snobbery, imitation, or attraction toward a new way of life. There are literally hundreds of African "intellectuals" who are living in the former European quarters of towns and who prefer Debussy or Bach to the music that can be heard in the "African" quarters, such as the Medina (Dakar), Nima (Accra), Treichville (Abidjan), New-Bell (Douala), or Poto-Poto (Brazzaville). African music will never develop unless these African "intellectuals" can be persuaded to take their own music seriously.

Obviously, preservation alone will never be able to attain the various objectives that we have listed. Preservation amounts to putting things into cold storage, whereas development means investment—investing in the corporate soul of the African people with a fair chance of making a profit, both in quality and in quantity.

However, as we have already underlined at the beginning of this book, African music will have no future if we ignore the musician who creates it. The musician needs to be constantly reminded that his music is essential and to be encouraged not to reject it. The most vital step is to assist him in the task of cherishing his art and spreading it around him. He is the teacher to whom the new African "schools of art" must turn if the African musical art is to be safeguarded. He must be encouraged to renew his ideas, for contrary to what some Europeans have written, the African musician can renew his conceptions. This is possible even though a civilization that is based on money and profit may put doubts in his mind. The musician alone can protect or rediscover the mystic force of his music. Only he can imbue it with all its vitality and dynamism, its brutality or tenderness—in short, its soul. He is the sole one who can perpetuate the communal aspect of music in Africa by inviting his people to gather around and participate in his songs.

The crux of the matter is to reach the people through the musician and to arouse public opinion by demonstrating the importance of the musician and his art. This is the sole positive means of approaching the dual aims of preservation and development. Neither can be achieved without the support of all of the people. It is they, after all, who are the only ones who know African music deeply; it has always been part of their existence. The participation of whole communities is the only way to guarantee the authenticity of the music whose preservation and development is at stake. Thus, the musician has an extremely

During this retreat they learn all they need to know in order to take their rightful place in adult society.

important coordinating role to play, not only as far as production and evolution are concerned, but also in the use of his art and in its integration into modern African life.

Musicians in many countries are well aware of this musician's role. Many of the social and political events that were unknown in Africa some thirty years ago have benefited from the participation of music. No electoral campaign would be complete without the active support of music. Take, for example, the two rival candidates in the Ibadan region of northwest Nigeria who decided to enlist the support of two rival groups of musicians in their electoral campaign. As a result some twenty-two 78 r.p.m. records were issued, one after another, in the course of a musical battle that occupied the two groups for several months during 1960. These records progressively revealed the programme and profession of faith of each candidate and served as a riposte to the insults and invectives that they hurled at one another. The seriousness of the campaign was in no way hampered by this musical presentation; on the contrary, the catchy dance music gave it an added dimension.

It would be hard to find a head of state in Africa who cannot claim that his governmental programme has been set to music, sung, or even danced. Musical tradition is making a serious attempt to keep abreast of the times and many current events are regularly set to music. The following song is a typical example of this kind of adaptation:

"Listen to me, you people whose land is poor; you people who can only rely on hunting to stay alive. Don't be impatient: the development plan will bring you irrigation and fertilizers to improve the soil. When all this has been achieved, you people will have to roll up your sleeves and work the land, to grow the grain which will give you a better life. You will have to organize cooperatives to ensure that your products are carefully controlled and sold at a fair price."[12]

This is an authentic *griot* song, performed by a young woman with a most delightful voice. Its total lack of poetry may appear mildly amusing, unless we stop to consider the far-reaching consequences it may have. It is no mean achievement if traditional music can convey in a harmonious and artistic manner the angular and sometimes difficult, modern message of the leaders to their people. In this musical form, the message will come much closer to the people and has a good chance of really being understood one day. Thanks to music, there is a real hope that these vital, new messages may be heard, accepted, and put into practice by the people. This will be a determining factor for the future of the African continent.

It is clear that African music goes far beyond the realm of art. And yet in these modern times, it manages to retain intact those of its former functions that have given African society throughout the ages its own particular character. This is a real capital, which is all the more precious because it is immutable. The formal elements of the music may change in order to keep abreast of the times and various new influences and although there may be some grounds for

Art of the past, which must relive today and prosper tomorrow, in a world which has need of it.

The Music

Two heads are better than one!

pessimism about the future of "authentic African music," its basic functions and deep significance are reassuringly stable.

It is this capital that Africans should take into account as they develop a new attitude that is adequately suited to modern times. They could, of course, deliberately limit themselves to maintaining the rich heritage of their own civilization which, despite the opinion expressed in non-African countries over many long centuries, is in no way inferior to that of the industrialized nations. Difficult as this limitation might be in the atomic age, it would be the only sure way to guarantee that the music of Africa would remain 100 percent African. But in the age of a dawning, worldwide civilization—and often the conflicts of differing ideologies and political systems are merely diverse reactions to the progressive encroachment of a universal civilization—the individuality of Africa can only assume its true value and fulfil its humanistic and humanitarian role if its culture is made accessible to all men.

This implicit paradox is a real challenge. It is indeed a paradox when initiation must retain all its power and inner value, even after its secret has been divulged. This enormous concession, however, is the price that has to be paid in order to enable the African mind to make a universal impact upon the non-African world.

Art is not a means but an end—transmutation from the human into the supernatural.

They emerge from the forest and their music and dancing, which everyone can understand, tells the world what initiation means.

The Music

Anyhow the future is here with its pretty muslin dresses . . . and its ancestral music.

Selective Discography

Revised and updated by Richard Hill.

AT THE TIME of going to press a number of recordings which fall within the area of this book may be found on the following labels available in Great Britain: *Afrotone, Anthology, Bären Reiter Musicaphon, Boîte à Musique, Folkways, Harmonia Mundi, Le Chant du Monde, Lyrichord, Nōnesuch (Explorer Series), Ocora, Philips, Tangent, Vogue.*

As stated below, the discography prepared for the English language edition of this book is based mainly on availability in the U.S.A. open market.

Information on availability in the U.K. may be obtained from:

Collet's Record Shop
70 New Oxford Street
LONDON W.C.1
Telephone: 01-636 3224

Discurio
International Record Store
9 Shepherd Street
LONDON W.1
Telephone: 01-493 6939

Or from the main U.K. distributor who would be willing to recommend a local dealer through which a particular recording could be obtained:

Continental Record Distributors Ltd.
97–99 Dean Street
LONDON W.1
Telephone: 01-437 1002

The choice of records that are featured in this discography is based on three criteria: documentary value; artistic quality; and availability on the open market in the U.S.A. Records that do not satisfy all three conditions have been omitted, even though they may be mentioned in the text, but the list is still sufficiently comprehensive to satisfy the requirements of the most exigent reader.

The discography is divided into four sections:

• Basic elements of a discography—a foundation on which to build a discography of traditional African music

- Classification by country (in alphabetical order)
- Classification by theme (from birth to funeral)
- Classification by groups and types of instrument

BASIC ELEMENTS OF A DISCOGRAPHY

The quantity and quality of commercial recordings of African music that are available today are such that it is not easy to select a few basic items that could be regarded as priority requirements for any reader who wishes to have his first glimpse of the black African musical world. Our choice is, therefore, deliberately limited to what we feel to be authentic and beautiful. We have attempted to do justice both to the art and to those who experience it. Each country in black Africa possesses its own musical treasures, each as true and valid as the rest. They all have the same destiny: to help man live. It is not, therefore, the country of origin that matters, but the musical content itself.

This content is often the same in various, far-distant countries, with slight variations in tone colour. For example, the *Massa* musician from Chad, singing the story of a journey, may recall the *Bamun* song, performed by the daughter of Sultan Njoya of Cameroon. Similarly, a Rwandese flute solo may have similarities with the music of the Sudanese *Fulani* shepherds. Such resemblances evidently confirm that there is a musical unity throughout black Africa; they are also an invaluable aid towards comprehension because they make the continent seem less vast and they give its music human dimensions.

For this reason, we feel that the reader should be recommended to purchase records that assemble recordings made in several different regions. They then may leave the study of music of one particular region for a second stage. Our proposed basic discography thus consists of the following items:

1. *Afrique Noire, panorama de la musique instrumentale* (*Panorama of the Instrumental Music of Black Africa*), BAM LD 409 A (see the section "Miscellaneous countries" in the classification by country).

2. *Les Ballets Africains de Keita Fodéba* (*Keita Fodeba's African Ballets*), Vogue LDM. 30.040 or LDM. 30.082 (see "Miscellaneous countries").

3. *Music of West Africa: Malinke* music (Guinea) and *Baule* music (Ivory Coast), Vogue Contrepoint MC 20.045 or Vogue LVLX–193.

COUNTRIES

Cameroon - Central African Republic - Chad - Congo and Zaire - Dahomey - Ethiopia - Gabon - Guinea - Ivory Coast - Lesotho - Madagascar - Mali - Niger - Nigeria - Rwanda - Senegal - Togo - Upper Volta - Miscellaneous countries.

CAMEROON

Danses et chants bamoun (*Bamun Dances and Songs*)

OCORA, SOR 3 - 12" LP. Recorded and presented by Louis C. D. Joos.

Side A: 1 - Victory song (four old warriors sing of the victorious return from a war against a neighbouring tribe); 2 - Epic song in honour of the *Bamun* kings (praise song); 3 - Young people's song (hope for an easier life); 4 - *Ndangie* Dance (song in praise of Sultan Njoya, 1896/1933, sung by the Sultan's daughter); 5 - *Banzie* Dance (war dance).

Side B: 1 - Njoya's Dance (invented by Sultan Njoya); 2 - Music for the Hanging of a Minister (see explanations on page 112); 3 - Nsangu's Dance (Sultan, 1860/1896); 4 - *Tikar* music (to entertain the king at mealtimes); 5 - Dance of the Princes and Princesses of the Royal Family (performed exclusively by members of the royal family, either at important festivals or prior to the funeral of a member of the royalty).

Musique fali, Nord-Cameroun *(Fali Music, North Cameroon)*

OCORA, SOR 9 - 10'' LP. Recorded and presented by Jean Gauthier.

Side A: 1 - Funeral music (''My friend, I should like to go with you to your grave'': song accompanied by a whistle ensemble and two drums—male and female principles); 2 - Mimed war song; 3 - Love song; 4 - Satirical song (''Your bean leaves smell odd''); 5 - Love song (for the daughter of a chief).

Side B: 1 - Flute solo; 2 - Music of the *kumbandji*, a clan of warriors (''One of the girls in my family has fallen into a pit''); 3 - Satirical song (''Why did you climb the mountain?''); 4 - Flute duet; 5 - Battle story; 6 - Song for the birth of twins.

Musiques du Cameroun *(Music of Cameroon)*

OCORA, OCR 25 - 12'' LP. Recorded by Tolia Nikiprowetzky, with the collaboration of the *Radiodiffusion nationale du Cameroun.* Commentary in English and French.

Side A: 1 - *Beti* xylophone (instrumental version of a song paying tribute to an old and distinguished person); 2 - *Bamileke* choir (women singers invite the young people of the village to be calm and obey the chief); 3 - *Bamileke* ensemble for the *kufo* (a secret funeral dance, reserved for princes or distinguished persons); 4 - *Bamileke* music (for the birth of twins); 5 - Royal *Bamun* dance; 6 - *Bamun* ensemble (dance music for the youth of the village).

Side B: 1 - *Bamileke* music for the *nekian* rite (performed once every two years for the coming of age of young people); 2 - *Bamileke* music (to honour an eminent guest); 3 - *Bamileke* mourning song; 4 - *Bakweri* funeral dance; 5 - *Bamileke* orchestra (music of rejoicing); 6 - *Bamileke* war dance (a secret dance reserved exclusively for the members of a secret society).

Chantefables du Cameroun *(Musical Fables of Cameroon)*

Le Chant du Monde LDZ-S 4326 - 10'' LP. Recorded and presented by S. Eno Belinga. The accompanying leaflet gives full details of the recordings. In connection with this record, see page 57 (*mvet* harp-zither).

CENTRAL AFRICAN REPUBLIC

République centrafricaine *(Central African Republic)*

OCORA, OCR ll - E.P. Recorded by Charles Duvelle, with the collaboration of Jean-Pierre Martin and Jacques M'Bilo of the *Radiodiffusion Centrafricaine.*

Side A: 1 - *Isongo* music (lament: ''Mother, why did you bring me into the world, which is so full of unhappiness?'' Accompanied by a large, ten-stringed *ngombi* harp, see page 50); 2 - *Gundi* music (orphans' song: ''We are lost and lonely, like chicks without their mother hen.'' Rhythmic accompaniment provided by a wicker rattle and wooden sticks struck together).

Side B: 1 - *Dakpa* music (two, five-keyed xylophones playing a musical initiation theme); 2 - *Mondjombo* music (song recounting the story of a man's life from birth to death).

Musique centrafricaine *(Music of the Central African Republic)*

OCORA, OCR 43 - 12'' LP. Recorded and presented by Charles Duvelle. Commentary translated into English by Josephine Bennett.

Side A: 1 - *Bagandu* music (excellent xylophone and *Sanza* duet, see *Sanza*, page 80 onwards, playing a most original piece of music whose theme is "The first wife is now last in her husband's heart"); 2 - *Babinga* music (Pygmy music, at the conclusion of a successful elephant hunt); 3 - *Linda* music (accompanying a very popular *Linda* dance); 4 - *Broto* music (horn ensemble playing initiation music, see page 68); 5 - Example of *N'dokpa* instrumental language (played on a four-keyed xylophone that can also be used for dance music—see following track); 6 - *N'dokpa* music (the four-keyed xylophone that was heard on the previous track for sending a message, here forms part of an orchestral ensemble playing dance music); 7 - *Dakpa* music (work song during the felling of a tree).

Side B: 1 - *Isongo* song (a young *Isongo* woman singing a lullaby in the evening, clapping her hands to provide a rhythmic accompaniment); 2 - *Azande* music (one xylophone, metal bells, and a single-headed drum play a lively dance rhythm); 3 - *Babinga* music (hunting music by two *Babinga* Pygmies, accompanied by a harp-zither and hand-clapping); 4 - *Dakpa* music (two men tap sticks together to imitate the sound of rain, in order to attract termites out of their ant-hill); 5 and 6 - *Bofi* children's songs ("In order to face life you must be careful" and "The wind has blown so hard it has uprooted the manioc"); 7 - *Bianda* music (song with eleven-keyed *Sanza* accompaniment: "If you don't want me any more, why don't you go away! . . .").

The Music of the Ba-Benzele Pygmies

Bären Reiter Musicaphon, BM 30 L 2303, Unesco Collection (Anthology of African Music) - 12'' LP. Recordings, commentary, and photographs by Simkha Aron in collaboration with Geneviève Taurelle. Commentary in German, English, and French.

Side A: 1 - *Hindewhu* whistle (return from a successful hunt; the *Ba-Benzele* use this whistle to announce the news to the women and old people who stayed in the camp); 2 - Song of rejoicing after returning from a hunt; 3 - *Nbou* (unaccompanied lament); 4 - *Kongo Asseka* ("The Girl with Breasts Small and Round like Wrists," music for dancing at a wake: two men's voices, women's choir, rattles, drums, and hand-claps); 5 - Song of rejoicing after a safe return from hunting; 6 - Lullaby (sung by a young *Benzele* woman, supporting her baby on her shoulder); 7 - Lullaby (performed by two women); 8 - *Ngoma*, the porcupine (an invocatory song before a hunt).

Side B: 1 - Song preceding the departure of the hunters; 2 - Music for entertainment (sung during a dance in which both men and women participate; three drums, two rattles, two pairs of ankle jingles, and hand-claps accompany the song); 3 - 7 - A series of stories in mime; a translation of these stories will be found in the commentary.

CHAD

Music of Kanem

Bären Reiter Musicaphon, BM 30 L 2309, Unesco Collection - 12'' LP. Recordings and commentary by Monique Brandily. Photographs by Max-Yves Brandily. Commentary in German, English, and French.

Side A: 1 - Professional drummers (Two drummers belonging to the caste of professional musicians—*griots*—play a set of three drums, one of which is a clay drum.); 2 - Song to drive birds into a trap (Two young boys—probably future *griots*—sing with the intention of luring birds into their nets.); 3 - Oboe solo (This oboe is rarely played alone; it is usually found in combinations with one or more drums. This example shows the technique used by African musicians that enables them to play extremely long phrases on the oboe, without the slightest interruption for breath, see page 77); 4 - Lullaby (sung by one girl); 5 - A set of drums (executed by three drummers on a pair of large, double-headed wooden drums; these drums are beaten only by adult men belonging to the artisan caste); 6 - Man's song accompanied on a one-stringed fiddle (traditional melody with the fiddle playing parallel to the voice); 7 - Reed clarinet solo (although the pipe has only one finger-hole, the player is able to produce four conjunct notes); 8 - Man's song accompanied on a drum (two-headed drum used exclusively by the descendants of prisoners); 9 - Song of *Tuareg* women (performed before the palace of the Sultan of Mao during the festival at the end of Ramadan).

Side B: 1 - Drums and rattles (music to summon the people of the village to a festival); 2 - Solo song of a woman (while working); 3 - Trumpet solo (see *Kakaki*, page 71); 4 - Man's song with lute accompaniment (lute with two metal strings. A praise song for a young chief who is told that from now on he will be obliged to give presents to musicians since he is his father's successor); 5 - Oboe solo (interpreted by the descendant of a captive who made the instrument himself. Note the Arabic influence.); 6 - Song of a young girl accompanied by hand-claps (responsorial song performed by a soloist and a chorus of women to accompany dancing); 7 - Ensemble of professional musicians (The ensemble is divided into two parts—a group of drums and an oboe and a singer accompanying himself on the lute. Such combinations are very frequent in this part of Chad); 8 - Festival at the end of Ramadan in Mao (an expression of collective jubilation by several groups of musicians, each consisting of an oboe and drums—in front of the Sultan's palace).

Anthologie de la musique du Tchad: (1) les Sara *(Anthology of the Music of Chad: (1) The Sara)*

OCORA, OCR 36 - 12'' LP. Recorded by Charles Duvelle and Michel Vuylstèke, with the cooperation of the *Radiodiffusion Nationale du Tchad*. Text, photographs, and production: Charles Duvelle. English translation by Josephine Bennett. This record is part of an album of three LP.s (OCR 36, 37, and 38) that obtained the *Grand Prix international du Disque de l'Académie Charles Cros* in 1968.

Side A: 1 - *Madjingaye* music (played after the harvest by an orchestra comprised of twelve bamboo whistles of differing sizes and two drums); 2 - *Madjingaye* music (song of initiation sung by a soloist and a choir of several dozen girls); 3 - *Madjingaye* music (danced by men in pairs, at certain festivities); 4 - *Nar* music (funeral song performed by a group of women).

Side B: 1 - *Gor* music (a xylophone with 14 keys and a drum accompany the dances of the initiates); 2 - *Gor* music (praises in honour of the traditional chief, sung by a singer accompanying himself on an eight-stringed bow-harp); 3 - *Kaba* music (festival music with xylophone, drums, rattle, and horn); 4 - *Doba* music (funeral song accompanied by two xylophones and two drums); 5 - *Kaba-Deme* music (This is used to encourage warriors. A solo musician sings and plays a xylophone with 13 keys. The instrument is placed on the ground with the keys almost perpendicular to the ground; the musician sits in front of the instrument and holds it in place by means of a strap).

Anthologie de la musique du Tchad: (2) le Mayo-Kebbi occidental *(Anthology of the Music of Chad: (2) Western Mayo-Kebbi)*

OCORA, OCR 37 - 12'' LP. See notes concerning the previous record, OCR 36.

Side A: 1 - *Massa* music (Two men sing this music as they return to the village with their flocks; without any break in the music, they make alternate use of the voice and a one-holed whistle); 2 - *Massa* music (sung by two women grinding millet); 3 - *Massa* music (description of a journey accompanied by three four-stringed bow-harps); 4 - *Mundang* music (dance music performed by a group of men in costume); 5 - *Mundang* music (the funeral ceremony of a woman healer).

Side B: 1 - *Tupuri* music (played before the harvest in the presence of the *chef de terre*); 2 - *Tupuri* music (played at harvest time; the orchestra consists of ten wind instruments); 3 - *Tupuri* music (to celebrate the harvest, interpreted by a singer and a wind ensemble); 4 - *Tupuri* music ("Each year, at different periods, but mainly during the dry season, the camps of the 'milk-drinkers' are formed. The men form into groups outside the village to follow a cure of cow's milk, which is supposed to make them strong and handsome . . . Their songs (of which this recording is an example) are particularly famed. Three large cylindrical drums with two skins and two horn whistles accompany the choir of milk-drinkers which, more than 50 in number, advances in a dense group, each man brandishing a stick.").

Anthologie de la musique du Tchad: (3) populations islamisées *(Anthology of the Music of Chad: (3) Islamic Populations)*

OCORA, OCR 38 - 12'' LP. See notes concerning record OCR 36, above.

Side A: 1 - *Barma* music (song to encourage the warriors before battle; a female singer, a rattle player, and four five-stringed bow-harp players—the harp is placed sideways so that the strings are parallel to the ground—play before a group of a dozen kneeling women, who perform a series of slow movements of the head, upper part of the body, and arms); 2 - *Barma* music (to encourage the canoeists and give them strength; three drums and two flutes); 3 - Arab *Dekakire* music (three-stringed lute to entertain young girls and encourage them to dance); 4 - Arab *Salamat* music (to accompany dances performed for amusement; three oblique flutes with four holes and three drums).

Side B: 1 - *Kanembu* music (music of praise by an orchestra composed of an oboe and three drums); 2 - *Mului* music (to greet a village chief; an oboe—called *ghaita* in Chad, three long trumpets of the *kakaki* type—known in Chad as *gachi*, and four drums. During this long sequence, which lasts 13', 40'', the oboe player performs without any discontinuation. See *alghaita*, page 76). This is without question the best recording of a traditional African orchestra, consisting of wind instruments played by professional musicians.

Percussions - Afrique No. 1: Tchad *(Percussions - Africa No. 1: Chad)*

OCORA, OCR 39 - E.P. Recorded by Charles Duvelle and Michel Vuylstèke, with the cooperation of the *Radiodiffusion Nationale du Tchad*.

Side A: Mbum music (rhythms performed during celebrations by a large open drum with one skin and a cylindrical drum with two laced skins).

Side B: Barma music (in honour of Sultan Ngaouran; an orchestra of three different kinds of drum).

CONGO and ZAIRE

Chants et danses pygmées *(Pygmy Songs and Dances)*

Le Chant du Monde LDY 4176 - 33 r.p.m. E.P. Recorded by C. Huchin and L. Demesse, among the *Ba-binga* Pygmies in the north of Congo-Brazzaville.

Side A: 1 - *Ebumba* dance (danced for entertainment as well as for acts of divination and healing; in the latter cases, it becomes a ritually complex magic or religious ceremony); 2 - *Evole* (bamboo whistle, played alternately with the musician's voice, see page 66 for details of this technique; see also "*The Music of the Ba-Benzele Pygmies*" Bären Reiter Musicaphon BM 30 L 2303, Side A, track 1, where the instrument is used in the same manner by the *Ba-Benzele* Pygmies); 3 - Hunting calls (imitations, using the nose and mouth, of antelope and monkey cries; attracted by what they take to be the sound of another animal of the same species the animals come within the range of the *assagai* or cross-bow in complete confidence); 4 - Tree felling (Pygmy song during the felling of a tree); 5 - Sung legend (telling the story of Mina and her mother who empty a pool to catch the fish in it. God, who lives in a nearby tree, is very angry and, after menacing Mina's mother, he kills her, chops her up and carries her off in his honey basket).

Side B: 1 - Song of the oarsmen (this is not a Pygmy song - the Pygmies cannot row - but is somewhat influenced by their music); 2 - Musical bow solo; 3 - Trumpet language (the trumpet repeats sentences spoken by a man); 4 - *Ekwose* (solo played on a three-stringed harp-zither of the *mvet* type); 5 - Family of drums ("father," "mother," and five "sons"); 6 - *Mobenga* dance (for entertainment).

Musique kongo *(Kongo Music)*

OCORA, OCR 35 - 12'' LP. Recorded in the *Kongo* region in the south-east of the People's Republic of the Congo (often referred to as Congo-Brazzaville). Recordings, photographs, and production: Charles Duvelle, with the technical cooperation of "The Voice of the Congolese Revolution". Assistant: Samuel Bicounou. English translation by Josephine Bennett.

Side A: 1 - *Ba-Bembe* children's songs (Three young boys sing and play an instrument that one of them has made. It is a sort of zither made from a long raffia stalk with one string on which two of the children beat a rhythm with wooden sticks, while the third boy moves a tin can full of pebbles, which acts as a resonator, along the string); 2 - *Ba-Lari* lullaby (accompanied by the rhythm of a *kodia* percussion-rattle, a large, snail shell filled with small pebbles); 3 - Musical recreation of *Ba-Lari* women (the rhythmic accompaniment is a combination of rattling percussion noises produced exclusively by the body); 4 - *Ba-Lari* song with three-stringed fiddle accompaniment (This fiddle is mentioned on page 44.); 5 - *Ba-Lari* lament with bow-lute accompaniment, see page 56; 6 - *Ba-Lari* walking song with *Sanza* accompaniment (typical utilization of the *Sanza*, which is the favourite accompaniment for walking songs, see page 80); 7 - *Ba-Bembe* sung narrative with five-stringed lute accompaniment.

Side B: 1 - Trumpet and percussion orchestra (seven ivory transverse trumpets, two double-headed kettledrums, and one bugle); 2 - *Ba-Congo-Nseke* drums (accompaniment to dancing, during the important ceremony which closes a period of mourning; the leading drum, *ngoudi*—the mother— has wax paste spread in the middle of its membrane, whose purpose is to regulate the frequency of the vibrations, see page 100); 3 - *Ba-Lari* orchestra with friction-drum, see page 100; 4 - *Ba-Bembe* horn ensemble (four wooden horns representing the father, mother, son, and daughter and two transverse horns made of wild coral tree roots, playing *bi-witi*, a piece of music which is heard only on rare occasions nowadays); 5 - *Ba-Bembe* choir and horns (same type of music as on the previous track).

Missa luba

Philips Standard B 14.723 - 12'' LP.

Side A: Missa Luba by the "Troubadours of King Baudoin," led by Father Guido Haazen. This interesting item is a mixture of European influences and Congolese musical traditions. The Mass itself—Kyrie, Gloria, Sanctus, Benedictus, Agnus Dei—is followed by versions of Ave Maria, Gloria in Excelsis Deo, and O Jesus Christ in which the synthesis of European and African music is unfortunately not quite so successful. The record is however well-worth hearing.

Side B: Savannah Mass (see Upper Volta).

Missa Kwango

Philips P 633.319 L - 12'' LP. "The Little Singers and Dancers of Kenge," directed by Father Bernard van den Boom. Another choir along the same lines as the "Troubadours of King Baudoin." A pleasant recording. The mass itself is followed by some 16 tracks, most of which are of a secular nature. Other records of this choir also exist.

Selective Discography

DAHOMEY

Musiques dahoménnes *(Music of Dahomey)*

OCORA, OCR 7 - 12'' LP. Recorded by Charles Duvelle of OCORA, with the collaboration of Michel Bakinde, Patient Chagas, and Janvier Ouangni of the *Radiodiffusion du Dahomey. Grand Prix de l'Académie du Disque Français - Prix de l'Institut de Musicologie* 1963–1964. English translation of text by Josephine Bennett.

Side A: 1 - *Nago* music (the music of a popular dance known as *Sakara*); 2 - *Nago* music (same orchestra as on the previous track, with the addition of singing); 3 - *Fon* music (*Hanye* was a type of music much appreciated at the court of the kings of Abomey); 4 - *Mahi* music (example of a *toba* raft-zither, see page 46); 5 - *Mahi* music (same *toba* orchestra as on the previous track, augmented by singing and hand-clapping); 6 - *Mahi* music (a piece chiefly played at funerals); 7 - *Somba* music (a piece played as a rule after the harvest); 8 - *Taneka* music (played during work in the fields); 9 - *Bariba* music (performed at the funeral of a fetisher).
Side B: 1 - *Dompago* music (played before circumcision to encourage those about to be initiated); 2 - *Yowabu* music (sings of the mighty deeds of a famous warrior, Kwiga. Accompanied by a musical bow with calabash resonator); 3 - *Dendi* music (praise songs); 4 - *Taneka* music (after the sacrifice of animals to the gods of the harvest); 5 - *Bariba* music (played at the enthronement of kings); 6 - *Bariba* music (leg-xylophone); 7 - *Bariba* music (during the funeral of a well-known hunter).

Ogoun dieu du fer *(Ogun, the god of iron)*

Vogue Contrepoint MC 20.159. New edition: Vogue LVLX–190 - 12'' LP. Recorded and presented by Gilbert Rouget.

Side A: Music for *Ogun*, the god of iron. This music is heard at the weekly ceremonies devoted to the cult of *Ogun*, one of the most important divinities of the *Nago* and *Yoruba* peoples.
1 - 3 - Greetings to the guardian of the sanctuary and calls to the divinities; 4 - 5 - Percussion and choir. Dances of the priests of *Ogun*.

Side B: Songs from various parts of West Africa.

Side B: 8 - Percussion for the *niegpadoudo* dance (sabre dance); 9 - Choir for the *whissegnikon* dance; 10 - Princes' choir; 11 - Priests' songs and dances for the sacrifice of a bull; 12 - ''Secret of the Vodun'' tune; 13 - *Asukablo* rhythm (to accompany one of the movements of the *Ablo*, a serpentine dance); 14 - *Niegpadoudo* rhythm.

ETHIOPIA

The Music of Ethiopia – Record II. Music of the Cushitic peoples of South-West Ethiopia.

Bären Reiter Musicaphon BM 30 L 2305, Unesco Collection - 12'' LP. Recordings and commentary by Jean Jenkins. Commentary in German, English, and French.

Side A: 1 - Flute ensemble (14 vertical bamboo flutes, each producing one note only); 2 - Praise song for the warriors, soloist, and chorus; 3 - Men's spear dance to celebrate the killing of a leopard; 4 - Prayer for rain (solo by a local chief); 5 - Celebration dance after a successful lion hunt; 6 - Personal history of an 82 year old man; 7 - Joking song in four-part canon, about the leading personalities in the village.

Side B: 8 - Boys' dance in praise of their friends; 9 - Personal history of a young man; 10 - Horn ensemble (for a wedding); 11 - One-stringed fiddle (*Masengo*) player singing the news; 12 -

Wedding dance; 13 - Coffee-grinding song; 14 - Fragment from the circumcision ceremony.

We have not included Record I of "The Music of Ethiopia" in the Unesco Collection (BM 30 L 2304) that is devoted to the music of the Coptic Church, because it has practically no connection with Negro-African musical tradition.

GABON

Musiques du Gabon *(Music of Gabon)*

OCORA, OCR 41 - 12" LP. Recorded among the *Fang, Kota, Masango, Njabi, Obamba, Punu,* and *Pgymies* of Gabon in January 1967. Recordings and photographs by Michel Vuylsteke of OCORA. Commentary translated into English by Josephine Bennett.

Side A: 1 - *Masango* mouth-bow (The *mungongo* musical bow is a sacred instrument used in the rites of the *bwiti*, religion widely practised in Gabon, especially in the east of the country. The sound of the *mungongo* symbolizes the voice of the divinities worshipped by the *bwiti* adepts); 2 - *Masango* funeral song (*Dissumba*, for the funeral of an old man, a member of the *bwiti* secret society. Accompanied by a *ngonfi* eight-stringed bow-harp, see page 50); 3 - *Fang* ensemble with xylophone (log xylophone, see page 84, used here during a ritual based chiefly on the cult of the dead); 4 - *Fang* xylophone orchestra (celebration music played by an orchestra of five xylophones, forming a keyboard with a total of 35 keys, accompanying a choir of girls with rattles); 5 - Epic song with *Fang mvet,* see page 57, harp-zither.

Side B: 1 - *Obamba* walking song (by four walkers); 2 - *Njabi* stilt dance (songs to accompany the movements of a masked dancer on stilts); 3 - *Punu* narrative song (with bow-lute accompaniment, see page 63, and rhythm provided by rods struck against a small beam laid on the ground and hand-clapping); 4 - *Kota* initiation music ("The *ongala* was a secret society whose initiation ceremony was accompanied by dances and songs. Originally only men and mothers of twins were allowed to be initiated . . . The initiation ceremonies took place at the time of the birth of twins, or during the funeral of a master of the secret society.") 5 - *Pygmy* song with harp (to accompany one of the dances of the *bwiti* secret society. The eight-stringed harp is played here with a rare virtuosity found in almost no other available harp recording: The prelude and finale are small masterpieces); 6 - *Pygmy* women's choir and drum (classical Pygmy songs with yodelling, to accompany dancing during a celebration; a dull-sounding drum and hand-clapping provide the accompaniment).

IVORY COAST

Musique baoulé, Côte d'Ivoire *(Baule Music, Ivory Coast)*

OCORA, OCR 34 - 12" LP. Recorded and presented by Charles Duvelle. Text translated into English by Josephine Bennett. An earlier edition of this record (SOR 6) obtained the *Grand Prix International du Disque, Académie Charles Cros* in 1962.

Sides A and B: Funeral ceremonies of a farmer; *Baule* songs and dances.

The Music of the Dan

Bären Reiter Musicaphon BM 30 L 2301, Unesco Collection - 12" LP. Recordings, commentary, and photographs by Hugo Zemp. Commentary in German, English, and French. *Grand Prix International du Disque, Académie Charles Cros* 1966.

Side A: 1 - Festival music; 2 - Solo song of a woman; 3 - Drum rhythms (at a circumcision festival); 4 - Music for a chieftain; 5 - Singing at a wrestling match; 6 - Sword dance of the young girls (concluding the excision rite); 7 - *Sanza* (portable instrument with plucked tongues); 8 - Song to encourage the rice sowers.

Side B: 9 - Singing game of small girls; 10 - Rice harvest; 11 - Music for the mask race; 12 - The mask *Baegbo*, see page 66, *mirlitons*; 13 - Trumpet orchestra; 14 - Dance of the women (after the successful birth of a child); 15 - Hunters' song from the savannah; 16 - Hunters' song from the forest.

The Music of the Senufo

Bären Reiter Musicaphon BM 30 L 2308, Unesco Collection - 12'' LP. Recordings, commentary and photographs by Hugo Zemp. Commentary in German, English, and French.

Side A: 1 - Xylophone orchestra; 2 - One-stringed harps (nine harps playing instrumental music and accompanying men's voices); 3 - Drums of the women (extremely rare in West Africa since women are generally not allowed to play drums); 4 - Flute ensemble of the chief; 5 - Men's song in the *Poro* language; 6 - Percussion instruments of the women (water-drums, see page 100); 7 - Trumpet orchestra (each producing only one or two notes; the melody results from blowing the instruments in alternation); 8 - Dance of the young people (each verse of the singer is answered by a xylophone); 9 - Song with iron rasps.

Side B: 10 - Song of the three young women (for their own entertainment); 11 - Orchestra for farm workers; 12 - Song of a woman grinding millet; 13 - Dance of the *Poro* initiates; 14 - Masked figures of the *Poro* (during funeral rites); 15 - Funeral rites for a member of the *Poro*. (The recordings present the most important sections of the music for the funeral rites, from the announcement of the death to the day of burial—extracts.)

Musique Guéré, Côte d'Ivoire *(Guere Music, Ivory Coast)*

Vogue LD 764 - 12'' LP. Recordings, notes, and photographs by Hugo Zemp.

Side A: 1 - Music for chopping down a tree (drums and chorus); 2 - Women's work song for hoeing a field; 3 - Forked-harp solo; 4 - Song by two old men who accompany themselves with gourd rattles; 5 - Young people's dance (singers, chorus, and two drums); 6 - Initiated girls' drum (''spoken'' drum messages alternate with unaccompanied singing); 7 - Mask's song (masked solo singer, chorus, gourd rattles, and whistle).

Side B: 1 - Song by two young women; 2 - Song accompanied by a harp-lu5e; 3 - Dance of a women's mask (chorus and drums); 4 - Xylophone music (a *Gbo* log-xylophone played by two musicians); 5 - War song (a singer with an iron bell and men's cries); 6 - Music of a secret society (a ''speaking'' slit-drum converses with a *mirliton*, followed by singing with orchestral accompaniment).

Masques Dan *(Dan Masks)*

OCORA, OCR 52 - 12'' LP. Recording, commentary, and photographs by Hugo Zemp.

The *Dan* have two kinds of mask—the usual kind consisting of men with a costume covering them entirely and a facial mask, and ''sound'' masks. ''Since the masks are considered by the *Dan* as supernatural beings they obviously neither speak nor sing with a human voice. But since they are incarnated by men, the men must change their voices into the voices of supernatural beings. The *Dan* have three ways of doing this. They distort their own voices, speak into an instrument which changes the quality of their voice or replace the human voice by sound instruments hidden from the uninitiated.''

Side A is devoted to ''dressed'' masks and *Side B* to ''naked'' masks.

MADAGASCAR

Musique malgache *(Malagasy Music)*

OCORA, OCR 24 - 12'' LP. Recorded by Charles Duvelle, with the collaboration of Michel Razakandraina of the *Radiodiffusion Nationale Malgache*.

Side A: 1 - Flutes and drums (open air music before a theatrical performance); 2 - Women's choir (song of praises during which homage is paid to various personalities); 3 - Song and *Lokanga Voatavo*, see page 46; 4 - Orchestra of *Mpilalao* (*Mpilalao* companies give performances combining music, dancing, theatre, and mime); 5 - Diatonic accordion (with rattle accompaniment); 6 - Lullaby.

Side B: 1 - Mixed choir (accompanying a healing rite); 2 - Whistles and choirs; 3 - Women's choir (song intended to encourage a boy about to be circumcised); 4 - Log xylophone, see page 84; 5 - Women's choir and conch; 6 - Choirs and musical bows (lament of a man who has lost his wife); 7 - Song by a man accompanying himself with an empty petrol can; 8 - Song before rice planting; 9 - *Beko* (a characteristic song from the south of the island, heard on various occasions, in particular during circumcision, funerals, etc.).

Valiha - Madagascar

OCORA, OCR 18 - 12" LP, see page 46. Recorded by Charles Duvelle (OCORA) and Michel Razakandraina (*Radiodiffusion Nationale Malgache*).

This record presents various aspects, sonorities, and uses of the *Valiha* zither as described on page 48. Once again, we should like to emphasize the interesting introduction to this record that gives a wealth of detail that was omitted from this book for reasons of balance.

MALI

Les Dogon *(The Dogon)*

OCORA, OCR 33 - 12" LP. *Grand Prix de l'Académie du Disque Français* 1958. Recorded by François Di Dio. Preface by Germaine Dieterlen. English translation by Josephine Bennett.

Side A: Songs of the Living: 1 - Dogon Greeting: *Ia Po* ("Greetings. Are you at peace? Yes, I am. And your wife? And your children? And the whole world? And the animals? . . .") 2 - Farmers' songs; 3 - Women's songs; 4 - Singers of *Sanga;* 5 - The grinding of the *Hogon's* millet (the *Hogon*, who is the oldest man in the village, acts as the religious leader); 6 - Song of the witchdoctors; 7 - *He! He! Yaoule mi obe ma he!* ("Where are you going to marry me? In the village of Baou? Or elsewhere? Where will you marry me?").

Side B: Funeral rites: 1 - The announcement of the funeral; 2 - Song of *Andoumboulou* (addressed to the spirits); 3 - The rhombus (bull-roarer); 4 - The bringing out of the masks; 5 - Dance of the *Kanangas* (large wooden masks in the shape of a Lorraine cross); 6 - The *Sirigue* dance (large mask over 20 feet high).

First Anthology of the Music of Mali

Bären Reiter Musicaphon BM 30 L 2501, 2502, 2503, 2504, 2505, and 2506. Produced by the Ministry of Information of Mali.

This series of six 12" LPs presents a panorama of the music of Mali:

Volume 1 - *The Steppes and Savannah of Mali (Mandingo* music)

Volume 2 - *Fluvial Mali (Peul* or *Fulani* music)

Volume 3 - *The Sands of Mali (Songhai* music)

Volume 4 - *The Ensemble Instrumental of Mali* (that obtained the Gold Medal at the Pan-African Cultural Festival of Algiers)

Volume 5 - *Ancient Strings - Batrou Sekou Kouyate* and *Sidiki Diabete,* two of the best *Kora* players of Mali are, as their names imply, *griots.*

Volume 6 - *Fanta Damba - The Epical Tradition -* "My repertory consists exclusively of ancient songs, most of which I learnt from my mother" - Fanta Damba, the celebrated singer from Mali.

NIGER

La musique des griots (*Music of the Griots*)

OCORA, OCR 20 - 12'' LP. Recorded by Tolia Nikiprowetzky with the cooperation of the *Radiodiffusion Nationale et du Haut Commissariat à l'Information de la République du Niger.*

Side A: 1 - *Sambalga (Sonrai* music: song with one-stringed fiddle accompaniment in memory of a famous *griot*); 2 - Work song for farmers *(Djerma* music: by a soloist and a choir of three men); 3 - Praise song in honour of the chiefs *(Djerma* music in honour of the successive chiefs of the region; three drums and an *alghaita*, see page 78, provide an instrumental accompaniment to the song); 4 - *Zatau (Djerma* magic song celebrating the genie *Zatau)*; 5 - *Babai* (another magic song, by *Mauri* musicians, invoking the genie *Babai*; accompanied by a one-stringed fiddle and two calabashes filled with gravel, shaken in rhythm); 6 - *Babai* (another invocation to the genie *Babai*, by a male soloist accompanying himself on a three-stringed lute); 7 - *Idina Mariana* (sung by *Ader* musicians who rattle metal rings together to provide a rhythmic accompaniment); 8 - *Agali* (another group of *Ader* musicians singing of *Agali,* a farmer of the region).

Side B: 1 - Song for the farmers *(Hausa* music by a group of eight singers, five of whom also play drums); 2 - *Bako (Hausa* music; *Bako* is the name of a celebrated hunter from the region of Kantche in Niger. His praises are sung here by an ensemble of musicians comprised of six lute players, five percussionists shaking calabashes containing pebbles, and a women's choir); 3 - *Sara (Hausa* music; *Sara* is a piece of music in honour of dead chiefs. The Chief's orchestra that plays here consists of 7 drums, 2 *Kakaki* and an *alghaita,* see page 71); 4 - *Dinari (Beri-Beri* music; instrumental prelude for various ceremonies; the orchestra is comprised of three drums and an *alghaita*; excellent example of the use of the *alghaita* to produce continuous sound, see page 64); 5 - Blacksmiths' song (male voice and one-stringed fiddle accompaniment played by the singer); 6 - *Mamani (Beri-Beri* music; dance song performed by a soloist accompanied by a women's choir and a drum); 7 - Dance music (recorded in *Beri-Beri* country; another example of the uninterrupted music of the *alghaita,* to a frenzied rhythm provided by three drums).

Nomades du Niger (*Nomads of Niger: music of the Tuaregs and the Bororos)*

OCORA, OCR 29 - 12'' L.P. Recorded and presented by Tolia Nikiprowetzky with the cooperation of the *Radiodiffusion du Niger.* Recording engineer: Innocent de Campos; photographs: Hasan Yacouba; text translated into English by Josephine Bennett.

Side A: Music of the Tuareg Women: 1 - *Ouane-Ouane*—song for the arrival of guests ("The sun has set, the moon has appeared. I can see the bright turbans of my guests who have come after dark to see me . . . ''); 2 - *Aboraki (* another song of praise of a type known as *tinde,* from the *tinde* drum used to provide the rhythm. Two women's voices take the solo part in turn, accompanied by a choir); 3 - *Ehayala-Ahane* (song of possession, to procure the healing of a sick man); 4 - *Henne-Amhee* (song which usually accompanies the men's dance; it belongs to the *ezele* style which, like the *tinde,* is particular to the *Tuareg* women).

Side B: (a) *Music of the Tuareg Men:* 1 - *Tikichkichene* ("Beautiful girls, this year I am sick, and my illness is neither a fever nor colic. It is simply because the year has passed me by without my shield having received a thrust from a sword which would have pierced it through and cut my leg''); 2 - *Tekalelt* (instrumental version of a love song, played on an *inzad*, one-stringed fiddle, see page 42); 3 - *Tailalt* (another love song, performed by a man accompanied by a one-stringed fiddle); 4 - *Ouenkalanine* (a very old tune played on an oblique flute with four holes, known in the Air of Niger as *sareoua*); (b) *Bororo music:* 5 - Love song (performed during a male beauty contest).

NIGERIA

The Music of Nigeria. Record I-Hausa Music

Bären Reiter Musicaphon BM 30 L. 2306, Unesco Collection - 12'' LP. Recordings, commentary and photographs by David Wason Ames. Commentary in German, English, and French.

Side A: 1 - Butchers' rhythm (a *Kalengu* hour-glass drum, see page 95, drumming up trade for his butcher patrons in the market place of Zaria); 2 - Singing and drumming in praise of blacksmiths *(Zaria)*; 3 - Praise song for a hunter (accompanied by a large, two-stringed lute called a *komo*, see page 46); 4 - Singing and drumming for farmers; 5 - Praise song for farmers; 6 - Royal drums of the *Emir* of Zaria (symbols of his high office).
Side B: 7 - Fanfare for the Sultan of Sokoto (three long trumpets—*Kakaki*—three single-reed oboes—*alghaita*—five horns, and two drums); 8 - Trumpet fanfare for the *Emir* of Zaria (to salute the *Emir* at daybreak); 9 - Horn and drum ensemble (the musicians of a District Head); 10 - Song in praise of Nigeria; 11 - Song celebrating the investiture of the *Emir* of Kano.

RWANDA

Music from Rwanda

Bären Reiter Musicaphon BM 30 L 2302, Unesco Collection - 12'' LP. Recordings and commentary by Denyse Hiernaux-l'hoest, photographs by Jacques Maquet. Commentary in German, English, and French.

Side A: *Tutsi Music*: 1 - Seven drums of the *mwami* (king) with song (the *ngoma* or royal drums represent power. The privilege of beating the royal drums was reserved for the aristocracy and transmitted from father to son); 2 - Song with hand-clapping (performed by men during nocturnal libations); 3 - Song of the spirits (celebration of the cult of *Ryangombe*, a legendary hero); 4 - Pastoral song (by a blind professional musician); 5 - Board zither, see page 46; 6 - Girl's song (a love song usually performed by groups of women at basket-making); 7 - Men's song with zither accompaniment; 8 - Six drums to wake the *mwami*; songs of praise of the sacred royal drums.

Side B: *Hutu Music* :9 - Vertical flute (pastoral music); 10 - singing with musical bow (historical tale); 11 - Song of the bride's friends; 12- Song with *likembe* accompaniment, see *Sanza*, page 80; 13 - Pastoral song; 14 - Two vertical flutes (representing the male and female who enter into a violent dispute); *Twa Music*: 15 - *Twa* orchestra; 16 - Song and dance (praise of an army corps); 17 - In praise of a chieftain (three women's voices).

SENEGAL

La musique des griots *(Music of the Griots)*
OCORA, OCR 15 - 12'' LP. Recorded and presented by Tolia Nikiprowetzky.
Side A: 1 - *Mansani*, played on the *Kora* (music commemorating the defeat of King Mansani Demba who was a traitor to his blood brothers); 2 - Song accompanied by *Kora* (the vocal art of the *griots* is well illustrated in this recording); 3 - *Wong* (war song with drum accompaniment); 4 - Beaten gourds (made from huge, dried, hollowed calabashes; they are placed on the ground and beaten with the hands to mark the rhythm); 5 - *Goumbe Samba* (song accompanied by beaten gourds, dedicated to the memory of a great *Serere* warrior); 6 - *M'Bare Gale* (typical *griot* song, accompanied on the fiddle, "All day long I have been roaming the neighbouring villages . . . ''); 7 - *Tanor Fatim Coura* (song by some elderly *griots*, whose average age is 60, in memory of a great warrior of the past); 8 - M'Babor (praise song for race horse owners); 9 - *Tara* (in the past women often used to sing *Tara* to their husbands when they returned from distant battles); 10 and 11

Percussion pieces; 12 - *Samba Bour N'Kaye* ("Oh Samba, king of the bush, you have travelled far across dunes and lakes to fetch the seed which will be exchanged for the oil, soap and oil-cake which are so necessary to us." See page 142).

Side B: 1 - *Inchallah* (song recorded in eastern Senegal, see page 113); 2 - *Lele* (sung by a poet-musician accompanying himself on a one-stringed lute: "Alas, everything here on earth is made to separate the lover from what he holds dearest"); 3 - Instrumental piece played on the *Molo*, one-stringed lute, see page 45; 4 - *Pekane* (song relating the exploits of the great fishermen who overcame the caïmans which used to infest the River Senegal); 5 - 6 - *Yela* (song of praise accompanied by beaten gourds); 7 - 8 - Pieces for two *Khalams* (lute duets); 9 - *Alioune Iba N'Diaye* (song to the glory of a famous wrestler).

TOGO

Musique kabré du Nord-Togo *(Kabre Music from Northern Togo)*.

OCORA, OCR 16 - 10" LP. Recorded and presented by Raymond Verdier.

Side A: 1 - Lithophone, see page 91; 2 - Two women's songs (first song: after finishing their domestic chores; second song: to encourage the hunters); 3 - Xylophone, see log xylophone, page 84; 4 - Burial (recorded on the way from the mortuary house to the grave); 5 - Funeral dance (among the *Kabre*, funerals of old men often take place six months or a year after death, in the dry season); 6 - Divination session (a soothsayer has been summoned to the house of the high priest to expose the ills which threaten the prosperity of the village land).

Side B: 1 - Rain dance (in the rainy season some *Kabre* honour the woman founder of their clan who gives them prosperity and fecundity with sacrifices and dancing); 2 - Song and whistles; 3 - Hunting song (a soloist alternates with a choir); 4 - Song of the *Efalas* (the *Efalas* are the first age-class of initiates); 5 - Dance of the *Kondanas* (the *Kondanas* are the initiates of the highest age-class, warriors aged between 25 and 30).

UPPER VOLTA

"Haute-Volta" *(Upper Volta)*

OCORA, SOR 10 - 10" LP. Recordings and photographs by Charles Duvelle. *Prix de l'Académie Charles Cros* 1962.

Side A: 1 - Orchestra of the *Naba* of Tenkodogo (traditional orchestra of twelve drums, belonging to the person of the *Naba* - traditional chief - accompanying the voice of a *griot* who majestically declaims the history of the *Nabas* of Tenkodogo, see page 104); 2 - *Bend Naba and Bila Balima* (another example of drums accompanying the words of a *griot* and transcribing the spoken words into rhythms); 3 - *Bambara* xylophone (with drum accompaniment. This music "speaks" in honour of the *Naba* of Tenkodogo); 4 - *Bumpa* (wind instrument with the sonority of the saxophone found in the *Bussance* region of Upper Volta and also among the *Dendi* of Dahomey who call it *Papo*, see "*Panorama of the Instrumental Music of Black Africa,* BAM LD 409 A, Side B, track 8); 5 - *Lontore* flute (an excellent recording of the transverse flute); 6 - *Bobal* (consists merely of a millet stalk with a slit at one end; *Fulani* shepherds are great virtuosi on this instrument).

Side B: 1 - Musical bow (love song played and accompanied by a single musician); 2 - *Lobi* xylophone (played by a blind musician while other people rattle small, metal rings. Very varied and engaging music); 3 - *Konde* lute (two-stringed lute "speaking" praises addressed to the village hunters); 4 - *Bussance* singers (praises to the chief of the village by two *Bussance* singers; they stop their ears to aid their concentration and their voices exude an intense, dramatic warmth); 5 - *Kone Sanza,* see *Sanza,* page 80 onwards.

See Ivory Coast. (This record is mentioned here even though all the recordings were actually made in the Ivory Coast because the *Senufo* region in fact covers the north of the Ivory Coast, the south-east of Mali, and the south-west of Upper Volta).

MISCELLANEOUS COUNTRIES

Les ballets africains de Keita Fodéba *(Keita Fodeba's African Ballets)*

Vogue LDM 30.040 - 12'' LP. Songs from various African countries.

Les ballets africans de Keita Fodeba, Vol 2 *(Keita Fodeba's African Ballets, Vol 2)*

Vogue LDM 30.082 - 12'' LP. Songs from various African countries.

"In composing the programmes of his famous African Ballets, Keita Fodeba's chief preoccupation is to avoid misleading the public by presenting images of a fictitious Africa. This is why he not only chooses songs from the traditional and pre-colonial Africa of his ancestors, but also those of modern Africa, which is gradually being marked by Western civilizaiton." (Quotation from the introduction to Vogue LDM 30.040, mentioned above. Our opinion of both these records, see page 56, coincides exactly with the above remarks.)

THEMES

Birth - Lullabies - Childhood; Games - Adolescence; Initiation - Love Songs - Marriage - Celebrations of Various Kinds - Laments - Praises - Farming - Miscellaneous Work - Satirical Songs - Court Music - War - Gods; Fetishism; Magic; Secret Societies - Death; Funerals.

BIRTH

Song for the birth of twins; *Fali* (North Cameroon): OCORA, SOR 9, *Musique fali,* Side B, track 6.

Bamileke music (Cameroon) for the birth of twins: OCORA, OCR 25, *Musiques du Cameroun,* Side A, track 4.

Dance of the women after the successful birth of a child; *Dan* (Ivory Coast): Bären Reiter Musicaphon BM 30 L 2301, *The Music of the Dan,* Side B, track 14.

LULLABIES

Ba-Benzele Lullabies (Pygmy; Central African Republic): Bären Reiter Musicaphon BM 30 L. 2303, *The Music of the Ba-Benzele Pygmies,* Side A, tracks 6 and 7.

Lullaby from Kanem (Chad): Bären Reiter Musicaphon BM 30 L. 2309, *Music of Kanem, Side A, track 4.*

Ba-Lari lullaby (Congo): OCORA, OCR 35, *Musique kongo,* Side A, track 2.

Malagasy lullaby (Madagascar): OCORA, OCR 24, *Musique malgache,* Side A, track 6.

CHILDHOOD–GAMES

Bofi children's songs (Central African Republic): "In order to face life you must be careful" and "The wind has blown so hard it has uprooted the manioc." OCORA, OCR 3, *Musique centrafricaine,* Side B, tracks 5 and 6.

Lito children's game (Central African Republic): an African version of "hunt the thimble."

Song to drive birds into a trap (Chad): Bären Reiter Musicaphon BM 30 L 2309, *Music of Kanem,* Side A, track 2.

Ba-Bembe children's songs (Congo): OCORA, OCR 35, *Musique kongo,* Side A, track 1.

ADOLESCENCE—INITIATION

Young people's song for a better life; *Bamun* (Cameroon): OCORA, SOR 3, *Danses et chants bamoun,* Side A, track 3.

Bamileke music for the *nekian* rite—the coming of age of young people (Cameroon): OCORA, OCR 25, *Musiques du Cameroun,* Side B, track 1.

Musical initiation theme; *Dakpa* (Central African Republic): OCORA, OCR 11, *République centrafricaine,* Side B, track 1.

Broto horn ensemble playing initiation music (Central African Republic): OCORA, OCR 43, *Musique centrafricaine,* Side A, track 4.

Girls' initiation song; *Madjingaye*; (Chad): OCORA, OCR 36, *Anthologie de la musique du Tchad,* Side A, track 2.

Gor xylophone music, with drums, accompanying the dances of the initiates (Chad): previous record, Side B, track 1.

Dompago music, played before circumcision to encourage those about to be initiated; (Dahomey): OCORA, OCR 17, *Musiques dahoméennes,* Side B, track 1.

Fragment from the circumcision ceremony; Cushite (Ethiopia): Bären Reiter Musicaphon BM 30 L. 2305, *The Music of Ethiopia II,* side B, track 14.

Kota intitiation music (Gabon): OCORA, OCR 41, *Musiques du Gabon,* Side B, track 4.

Dance of the young girls, concluding the excision rite; *Dan* (Ivory Coast): Bären Reiter Musicaphon BM 30 L 2301, *The Music of the Dan,* Side A, track 6.

The mask *Baegbo; Dan* (Ivory Coast): previous record, Side B, track 12.

Women's choir to encourage a boy about to be circumcised (Madagascar): OCORA, OCR 24, *Musique malgache,* Side B, track 3.

Songs of *Kabre* initiates (Northern Togo): OCORA, OCR 16, *Musique kabrè du Nord-Togo,* Side B, tracks 4 and 5.

LOVE SONGS

Fali love songs (Cameroon): OCORA, SOR 9, *Musique fali, Nord-Cameroun,* Side A, tracks 3 and 5.

Tekalelt, instrumental version of a love song played on the one-stringed fiddle (Niger): OCORA, OCR 29, *Nomades du Niger,* Side B, track 2.

Bororo love song (Niger): previous record, Side B, track 5.

Tutsi girl's song (Rwanda): Bären Reiter Musicaphon BM 30 L 2302, *Music from Rwanda,* Side A, track 6.

Lele, love song with one-stringed lute accompaniment (Senegal): OCORA, OCR 15, *Sénégal, la musique des griots,* Side B, track 2.

Love song with musical bow accompaniment (Upper Volta): OCORA, SOR 10, *Haute-Volta,* Side B, track 1.

MARRIAGE

Wedding dance; Cushite (Ethiopia): Bären Reiter Musicaphon BM 30 L 2305, *The Music of Ethiopia II,* Side B, Track 12.

Song of the bride's friends; *Hutu (*Rwanda): Bären Reiter Musicaphon BM 30 L 2302, *Music from Rwanda,* Side B, track 11.

CELEBRATIONS OF VARIOUS KINDS

Dance of the Princes and Princesses of the Royal Family; *Bamun* (Cameroon): OCORA, SOR 3, *Danses et chants bamoun,* Side B, track 5.

Bamun ensemble, dance music for the youth of the village (Cameroon): OCORA, OCR 25, *Musiques du Cameroun,* Side A, track 6.

Bamileke music of rejoicing (Cameroon): previous record, Side B, track 5.

Babinga Pygmy music, at the conclusion of a successful elephant hunt (Central African Republic): OCORA, OCR 43, *Musique centrafricaine,* Side A, track 2.

Songs of rejoicing after returning from a hunt; *Ba-Benzele Pygmy* (Central African Republic): Bären Reiter Musicaphon BM 30 L 2303, *The Music of the Ba-Benzele Pgymies,* Side A, tracks 2 and 5.

Song of *Tuareg* women, during the festival of Ramadan (Chad): Bären Reiter Musicaphon BM 30 L 2309, *Music of Kanem,* Side A, track 9.

Drums and rattles, to summon the villagers to a festival (Chad): previous record, Side B, track 10.

Festival at the end of Ramadan in Mao (Chad): previous record, Side B, track 17.

Madjingaye music, danced by men in pairs at certain festivities (Chad): OCORA, OCR 36, *Anthologie de la musique du Tchad,* Side A, track 3.

Kaba festival music (Chad): previous revord, Side B, track 3.

Mundang dance music (Chad): OCORA, OCR 37, *Anthologie de la musique du Tchad,* Side A, track 4.

Tupuri music to celebrate the harvest (Chad): previous record, Side B, track 3.

Music of the *Tupuri* milk-drinkers (Chad): previous record, Side B, track 4.

Arab *Salamat* music to accompany dances performed for amusement (Chad): OCORA, OCR 38, *Anthologie de la musique du Tchad,* Side A, track 4.

Ba-Congo-Nseke drums to accompany dancing (Congo): OCORA, OCR 35, *Musique kongo,* Side B, track 2.

Nago music, a popular dance known as *Sakara* (Nigeria and Dahomey): OCORA, OCR 17, *Musiques dahoméennes,* Side A, track 1.

Bariba music played at the enthronement of kings (Dahomey): previous record, Side B, track 5.

Celebration dance after a successful lion hunt; Cushite (Ethiopia): Bären Reiter Musicaphon BM 30 L 2305, *The Music of Ethiopia II,* Side A, track 5.

Fang xylophone orchestra playing celebration music (Gabon): OCORA, OCR 41, *Musiques du Gabon,* Side A, track 4.

Pygmy women's choir and drum, to accompany dancing during a celebration (Gabon): previous record, Side B, track 6.

Beri-Beri dance music (Niger): OCORA, OCR 20, *Niger - la musique des griots,* Side B, track 7.

Hutu song and dance (Rwanda): Bären Reiter Musicaphon BM 30 L 2302, *Music from Rwanda,* Side B, track 16.

LAMENTS

Isongo music (Central African Republic): OCORA, OCR 11, *République centrafricaine,* Side A, track 1.

Gundi orphans' song (Central African Republic): previous record, Side A, track 2.

Unaccompanied lament (Central African Republic): Bären Reiter Musicaphon BM 30 L 2303, *The Music of the Ba-Benzele Pygmies,* Side A, track 3.

Ba-Lari lament with bow-lute accompaniment (Congo) OCORA, OCR 35, *Musique kongo,* Side A, track 5.

Lament of a man who has lost his wife (Madagascar): OCORA, OCR 24, *Musique malgache,* Side B, track 6.

PRAISES

In Praise of God

Luba songs (Congo): Philips B 14 723 L, *Missa Luba,* Side A.
Kwango songs (Congo): Philips P 633 319 L, *Missa kwango,* Sides A and B.

In Praise of Kings, Chiefs, Lords or other Dignitaries

Epic song in honour of the *Bamun* kings (Cameroon): OCORA, SOR 3, *Danses et chants bamoun,* Side A, track 2.

Song in praise of Sultan Njoya; *Bamun (Cameroon):* previous record, Side A, track 4.

Beti xylophone, paying tribute to an old and distinguished person (Cameroon): OCORA, OCR 25, *Musiques du Cameroun,* Side A, track 1.

Bamileke music to honour an eminent guest (Cameroon): previous record, Side B, track 2.

Gor music, praises in honour of the traditional chief (Chad): OCORA, OCR 36, *Anthologie de la musique du Tchad,* Side B, track 2.

Music for a *Dan* Chieftain (Ivory Coast): Bären Reiter Musicaphon BM 30 L 2301, *The Music of the Dan,* Side A, track 4.

Djerma praise song in honour of the chiefs (Niger): OCORA, OCR 20, *La musique des griots - Niger,* Side A, track 3.

Hausa music in honour of dead chiefs (Niger): previous record, Side B, track 3.

Tutsi music in honour of the *mwami* (Rwanda): Bären Reiter Musicaphon BM 30 L 2302, *Music from Rwanda,* Side A, track 8.

Twa music in praise of a chieftain (Rwanda): previous record, Side B, track 17.

Orchestra of the *Naba*—traditional chief—of Tenkodogo (Upper Volta): OCORA, SOR 10, *Haute-Volta,* Side A, tracks 1 and 2.

Bussance musicians singing praises to the chief of the village (Upper Volta): previous record, Side B, track 4.

In Praise of Trades and Corporations

Kanembu music of praise by an orchestra composed of an oboe and three drums (Chad): OCORA, OCR 38, *Anthologie de la musique du Tchad,* Side B, track 1.

Yowabu music singing of the mighty deeds of a famous warrior, *Kwiga* (Dahomey): OCORA, OCR 17, *Musiques dahoméennes,* Side B, track 2.

Praise song for the warriors; Cushite (Ethiopia): Bären Reiter Musicaphon BM 30 L 2305, *The Music of Ethiopia II,* Side A, track 2.

Song for *Agali*, a farmer of an *Ader* village (Niger): OCORA, OCR 20, *La musique des griots - Niger,* Side A, track 8.

Song for the farmers; *Hausa* (Niger): previous record, Side B, track 1.

Music for *Bako,* a celebrated hunter from the region of Kantche; *Hausa* (Niger): previous record, Side B, track 2.

Blacksmiths' song (Niger): previous record, Side B, track 5.

Singing and drumming in praise of blacksmiths; *Hausa (* Nigeria): Bären Reiter Musicaphon BM 30 L 2306, *The Music of Nigeria: I. Hausa Music,* Side A, track 2.

Praise song for a hunter; *Hausa* (Nigeria): previous record, Side A, track 3.

Praise song for farmers; *Hausa* (Nigeria): previous record, Side A, track 5.

Praise of an army corps; *Hutu* music (Rwanda): Bären Reiter Musicaphon BM 30 L 2302, *Music from Rwanda,* Side B, track 16.

Praise song for racehorse owners (Senegal); previous record, Side A, track 8.

Song dedicated to the memory of a great *Serere* warrior (Senegal):OCORA, OCR 15, *La musique des griots - Sénégal,* Side A, track 5.

Song in honour of the fishermen who overcame the caïmans that used to infest the River Senegal (Senegal): previous record, Side B, track 4.

Song to the glory of a famous wrestler (Senegal): previous record, Side B, track 9.

Konde lute singing praises to the village hunters (Upper Volta): OCORA, SOR 10, *Haute-Volta*, Side B, track 3.

FARMING

Madjingaye music played after the harvest (Chad): OCORA, OCR 36, *Anthologie de la musique du Tchad*, Side A, track 1.

Tupuri music played before the harvest (Chad): OCORA, OCR 37, *Anthologie de la musique du Tchad*, Side B, track 1.

Tupuri music played at harvest time (Chad): previous record, Side B, track 2.

Tupuri music to celebrate the harvest (Chad): previous record, Side B, track 3.

Somba music usually played after the harvest (Dahomey): OCORA, OCR 17, *Musiques dahoméennes*, Side A, track 7.

Taneka music played during work in the fields (Dahomey): previous record, Side A, track 8.

Song to encourage the rice sowers; *Dan* (Ivory Coast): Bären Reiter Musicaphon BM 30 L 2301, *The Music of the Dan*, Side A, track 8.

Rice harvest; *Dan* (Ivory Coast): previous record, Side B, track 10.

Orchestra for farm workers; *Senufo* (Ivory Coast): Baren Reiter Musicaphon BM 30 L 2308, *The Music of the Senufo*, Side B, track 2.

Song before planting rice (Madagascar): OCORA, OCR 24, *Musique malgache, Side B, track 8.*

Work song for farmers; Djerma (Niger): OCORA, OCR 20, *La musique des griots - Niger*, Side A, track 2.

Song for the farmers; *Hausa* (Niger): previous record, Side B, track 1.

Praise song for farmers; *Hausa* (Nigeria): Bären Reiter Musicaphon BM 30 L 2306, *The Music of Nigeria: I. Hausa Music*, Side A, track 5.

MISCELLANEOUS WORK

Dakpa work song, during the felling of a tree (Central African Republic): OCORA, OCR 43, *Musique centrafricaine*, Side A, track 7.

Massa song by women grinding millet (Chad): OCORA, OCR 37, *Anthologie de la musique du Tchad*, Side A, track 2.

Barma music to encourage the canoeists and give them strength (Chad): OCORA, OCR 38, *Anthologie de la musique du Tchad*, Side A, track 2.

Pygmy song during the felling of a tree (Congo): Le Chant du Monde LDY 4176, *Chants et danses pygmées*, Side A, track 4.

Song of the oarsmen (Congo): previous record, Side B, track 1.

Coffee-grinding song; Cushite (Ethiopia): Bären Reiter Musicaphon BM 30 L 2305, *The Music of Ethiopia II*, Side B, track 13.

Hunters' songs, from the savannah and from the forest; *Dan* (Ivory Coast): Bären Reiter Musicaphon BM 30 L 2301, *The Music of the Dan*, Side B, tracks 15 and 16.

Song of a woman grinding millet; *Senufo* (Ivory Coast): Bären Reiter Musicaphon BM 30 L 2308, *The Music of the Senufo*, Side B, track 12.

The grinding of the *Hogon's* millet; *Dogon* (Mali): OCORA, OCR 33, *Les Dogon*, Side A, track 5.

Blacksmiths' song, male voice and one-stringed fiddle accompaniment (Niger): OCORA, OCR 20, *La musique des griots - Niger*, Side B, track 5.

Butcher's rhythm; *Hausa* (Nigeria): Bären Reiter Musicaphon BM 30 L 2306, *The Music of Nigeria: I. Hausa Music*, Side A, track 1.

Singing and drumming for farmers; *Hausa* (Nigeria): previous record, Side A, track 4.

Tutsi pastoral song (Rwanda): Bären Reiter Musicaphon BM 30 L 2302, *Music from Rwanda*, Side A, track 4.

Hutu pastoral song (Rwanda): previous record, Side B, track 13.

Kabre hunting song (Togo): OCORA, OCR 16, *Musique kabrè du Nord-Togo*, Side B, track 3.

SATIRICAL SONGS

Fali satirical song Cameroon): OCORA, OCR 9, *Musique fali, Nord-Cameroun,* Side A, track 4.

Fali satirical song (Cameroon): previous record, Side B, track 3.

Instrumental version of a *Bagandu* satirical song (Central African Republic): OCORA, OCR 43, *Musique centrafricaine,* Side A, track 1.

Bianda satirical song, with *Sanza* accompaniment (Central African Republic): previous record, Side B, track 7.

Joking song in four-part canon; Cushite (Ethiopia): Bären Reiter Musicaphon BM 30 L 2305, *The Music of Ethiopia II,* Side A, track 7.

Satirical song with forked harp accompaniment; *Baule* (Ivory Coast): Vogue Contrepoint MC20.045 or Vogue LVLX - 193, *Music of West Africa,* Side B, track 5.

COURT MUSIC

Epic song in honour of the *Bamun* kings (Cameroon): OCORA, SOR 3, *Danses et chants bamoun,* Side A, track 2.

Ndangie dance; *Bamun* (Cameroon): previous record, Side A, track 4.

Banzie dance; *Bamun* (Cameroon): previous record, Side A, track 5.

Njoya's dance; *Bamun* (Cameroon): previous record, Side B, track 1.

Music for the hanging of a minister; *Bamun* (Cameroon): previous record, Side B, track 2.

Nsangu's dance; *Bamun* (Cameroon): previous record, Side B, track 3.

Tikar music to entertain the king at mealtimes (Cameroon): previous record, Side B, track 4.

Dance of the Princes and Princesses of the Royal Family; *Bamun* (Cameroon): previous record, Side B, track 5.

Fon music: *Hanye,* a type of music much appreciated at the court of the kings of Abomey (Dahomey): OCORA, OCR 17, *Musiques dahoméennes,* Side A, track 3.

Bariba music played at the enthronement of kings (Dahomey): previous record, Side B, track 5.

Royal drums of the *Emir* of Zaria (Nigeria): Bären Reiter Musicaphon BM 30 L 2306, *The Music of Nigeria: I. Hausa Music,* Side A, track 6.

Fanfare for the Sultan of Sokoto (Nigeria): previous record, Side B, track 7.

Trumpet fanfare for the *Emir of* Zaria (Nigeria): previous record, Side B, track 8.

Song celebrating the investiture of the *Emir* of *Kano* (Nigeria): previous record, Side B, track 11.

Rukina, praises to the *Tutsi* king (Rwanda): Bären Reiter Musicaphon BM 30 L 2302, *Music from Rwanda,* Side A, track 1.

Tutsi court music (Rwanda): previous record, Side A, track 8.

Orchestra of the *Naba* of Tenkodogo (Upper Volta): OCORA, SOR 10, *Haute-Volta,* Side A, tracks 1 and 2.

WAR

Victory song, by four old *Bamun* warriors (Cameroon): OCORA, SOR 3, *Chants et Danses bamoun,* Side A, track 1.

Banzie, war dance; *Bamun* (Cameroon): previous record, Side A, track 5.

Mimed war song; *Fali* (Cameroon): OCORA, SOR 9, *Musique fali, Nord-Cameroun,* Side A, track 2.

Barma music to encourage warriors before battle (Chad): OCORA, OCR 38, *Anthologie de la musique du Tchad*, Side A, track 1.

Praise song for the warriors; Cushite (Ethiopia): Bären Reiter Musicaphon BM 30 L 2305, *The Music of Ethiopia II*, Side A, track 2.

Praise of an army corps; *Hutu* (Rwanda): Bären Reiter Musicaphon BM 30 L 2302, *Music from Rwanda*, Side B, track 16.

War song with drum accompaniment (Senegal): OCORA, OCR 15, *Sénégal - la musique des griots*, Side A, track 3.

Song dedicated to the memory of a great *Serere* warrior (Senegal): previous record, Side A, track 5.

Song by elderly *griots*, in memory of a great warrior of the past (Senegal): previous record, Side A, track 7.

Song sung by women to welcome back their husbands from distant battles (Senegal): previous record, Side A, track 9.

GODS - FETISHISM - MAGIC - SECRET SOCIETIES
(See Also Adolescence; Initiation)

Bamileke ensemble for the *kufo*, secret funeral dance reserved for princes or distinguished persons (Cameroon): OCORA, OCR 25, *Musiques du Cameroun*, Side A, track 3.

Bamileke war dance, reserved exclusively for the members of a secret society (Cameroon): previous record, Side B, track 6.

Invocatory song before a hunt; *Ba-Benzele* Pygmy (Central African Republic): Bären Reiter Musicaphon BM 30 L 2303, *The Music of the Ba-Benzele Pygmies*, Side A, track 8.

Divination or healing dance; *Babinga* Pygmy (Congo): Le Chant du Monde LDY 4176, *Chants et danses pygmeés*, Side A, track 1.

Taneka music, after the sacrifice of animals to the gods of the harvest (Dahomey): OCORA, OCR 17, *Musiques dahoméennes*, Side B, track 4.

Prayer for rain; Cushite (Ethiopia): Bären Reiter Musicaphon BM 30 L 2305, *The Music of Ethiopia II*, Side A, track 4.

Masango mouth-bow used in the rites of the *bwiti*, a religion widely practised in Gabon (Gabon): OCORA, OCR 41, *Musiques du Gabon*, Side A, track 1.

Fang xylophone ensemble used during a ritual based chiefly on the cult of the dead (Gabon): previous record, Side A, track 3.

Pygmy song with harp to accompany one of the dances of the *bwiti* secret society (Gabon): previous record, Side B, track 5.

Zatau, Djerma magic song (Niger): OCORA, OCR 20, *Niger - la musique des griots*, Side A, track 4.

Two songs invoking a genie, *Babai; Mauri* (Niger): previous record, Side A, tracks 5 and 6.

Song of possession, to procure the healing of a sick man; *Tuareg* (Niger): OCORA, OCR 29, *Nomades du Niger*, Side A, track 3.

Song of the spirits; *Tutsi* (Rwanda): Bären Reiter Musicaphon BM 30 L 2302, *Music from Rwanda*, Side A, track 3.

Divination session; *Kabre* (Togo): OCORA, OCR 16, *Musique kabrè du Nord-Togo*, Side A, track 6.

Rain dance; in the rainy season some *Kabre* honour the woman founder of their clan (Togo): previous record, Side B, track 1.

DEATH - FUNERALS

Fali funeral music (Cameroon): OCORA, SOR 9, *Musique fali, Nord-Cameroun*, Side A, track 1.

Bamileke mourning song (Cameroon): OCORA, OCR 25, *Musiques du Cameroun*, Side B, track 3.

Bakweri funeral dance (Cameroon): previous record, Side B, track 4.

Nar funeral song (Chad): OCORA, OCR 36, *Anthologie de la musique du Tchad,* Side A, track 4.

Doba funeral song (Chad): previous record, Side B, track 4.

Funeral ceremony of a woman healer; *Mundang* (Chad): OCORA, OCR 37, *Anthologie de la musique du Tchad,* Side A, track 5.

Mahi funeral music (Dahomey): OCORA, OCR 17, *Musiques dahoméennes,* Side A, track 6.

Bariba music performed at the funeral of a fetisher (Dahomey): previous record, Side A, track 9.

Bariba music during the funeral of a well-known hunter (Dahomey): previous record, Side B, track 7.

Masango funeral song, for the funeral of an old man, a member of the *bwiti* secret society (Gabon): OCORA, OCR 41, *Musiques du Gabon,* Side A, track 2.

Funeral ceremonies of a farmer; *Baule* (Ivory Coast): OCORA, OCR 34, *Musique baoulé.*

Masked figures during funeral rites; *Senufo* (Ivory Coast): Bären Reiter Musicaphon BM 30 L 2308, *The Music of the Senufo,* Side B, track 14.

Funeral rites for a member of the *Poro; Senufo* (Ivory Coast): previous record, Side B, track 15.

Lament of a man who has lost his wife (Madagascar): OCORA, OCR 24, *Musique malgache,* Side B, track 6.

Dogon funeral rites (Mali): OCORA, OCR 33, *Les Dogon,* Side B.

Hausa music in honour of dead chiefs (Niger): OCORA, OCR 20, *Niger - la musique des griots,* Side B, track 3.

Kabre burial (Togo): OCORA, OCR 16, *Musique kabrè du Nord-Togo,* Side A, track 4.

Kabre funeral dance (Togo): previous record, Side A, track 5.

GROUPS AND TYPES OF INSTRUMENT

Stringed Instruments - Wind and Air Instruments - Keyboard Instruments - Lithophones - Drums.

STRINGED INSTRUMENTS

Fiddles, see page 41.

Bären Reiter Musicaphon BM 30 L 2305, *The Music of Ethiopia II,* Side B, track 11: One-stringed fiddle-player singing the news.

OCORA, OCR 15, *Sénégal, la musique des griots,* Side A, track 6: Song for male voice, with *Riti* one-stringed fiddle accompaniment.

OCORA, OCR 17, *Musiques dahoméennes,* Side A, tracks 1 and 2: Orchestra and song, with *Godie* fiddle.

OCORA, OCR 20, *Niger, la musique des griots,* Side A, track 5: Magic song with fiddle accompaniment.

OCORA, OCR 29, *Nomades du Niger,* Side B, track 2: *Inzad* fiddle solo; Side B, track 3: Song with fiddle accompaniment.

OCORA, OCR 35, *Musique kongo,* Side A, track 4: Song with three-stringed fiddle accompaniment.

Lutes, see page 45.

One-stringed lute:

OCORA, OCR 15, *Sénégal, la musique des griots,* Side B, track 3: *Molo* one-stringed lute solo; Side B, track 2: Song with *Molo* accompaniment.

Two-stringed lute:

Bären Reiter Musicaphon BM 30 L 2306, *The Music of Nigeria: I. Hausa Music,* Side A, track 3: Praise song for a hunter, accompanied by a *komo* two-stringed lute.

OCORA, SOR 10, *Haute-Volta,* Side B, track 3: Two-stringed lute (*Konde*) ''speaking'' praises addressed to the village hunters.

Three-stringed lute:

OCORA, OCR 20, *Niger, la musique des griots,* Side A, track 6: Invocation to the genie *Babai,* accompanied by a three-stringed lute.

OCORA, OCR 38, *Anthologie de la musique du Tchad*, Side A, track 3: Music to entertain young girls and encourage them to dance, played on a *djigendi algara* three-stringed lute.

Zithers, see page 46.
Bären Reiter Musicaphon BM 30 L 2302, *Music from Rwanda*, Side A, track 5: *Inanga* (Rwandese zither) solo.
OCORA, OCR 17, *Musiques dahoméennes*, Side A, tracks 4 and 5: Orchestra with *toba* raft-zither.
OCORA, OCR 18, *Valiha - Madagascar*, the whole record is devoted to the *valiha* tubular zither.
OCORA, OCR 24, *Musique malgache*, Side A, track 3: Song accompanied by a *lokanga voatavo* zither.

Harps, see page 50.
Bären Reiter Musicaphon BM 30 L 2308, *The Music of the Senufo*, Side A, track 2: One-stringed harp music.
OCORA, OCR 37, *Anthologie de la musique du Tchad*, Side A, track 3: Song accompanied by three four-stringed bow-harps known as *dilla*.
OCORA, OCR 38, *Anthologie de la musique du Tchad*, Side A, track 1: *Kinde* five-stringed bow-harp, placed on the ground sideways.
Vogue Contrepoint MC 20.141, *Pondo Kakou, musique de société secrète*, Side B, track 8: *Bolon* three-stringed harp duet (Guinea).
Vogue LDM 30.082, *Les Ballets africains de Keita Fodeba*, Side A, track 2: Praise song accompanied on the *Kora*.

Mvet Harp-zither, see page 44.
Le Chant du Monde LDZ-S 4326, *Chantefables du Cameroun*, see page 57.
OCORA, SOR 3, *Danses et chants bamoun*, Side A, track 3: Young people's song with *mvet* accompaniment.
OCORA, OCR 12, *Musique centrafricaine*, Side B, track 3: Pygmy harp-zither.

Bow-lutes and Musical bows, see page 63.
OCORA, OCR 35, *Musique kongo*, Side A, track 5: Bow-lute.
OCORA, OCR 17, *Musiques dahoméennes*, Side B, track 2, *Tiepore* musical bow.
OCORA, OCR 24, *Musique malgache*, Side B, track 6: Resonator-bow.
Bären Reiter Musicaphon BM 30 L 2302, *Music from Rwanda*, Side B, track 2: Resonator-bow accompanying a historical tale.

WIND AND AIR INSTRUMENTS

Mirlitons, see page 64.
Bären Reiter Musicaphon BM 30 L 2301, *The Music of the Dan*, Side B, track 12: "The Mask Baegbo", a group of *mirlitons* that constitute an acoustic mask, used in certain ancient rites.

Whistles, see 66.
Bären Reiter Musicaphon BM 30 L 2303, *The Music of the Ba-Benzele Pygmies*, Side A, track 1: Music of rejoicing after the return from a successful hunt: The whistle alternates with the player's voice.
OCORA, OCR 37, *Anthologie de la musique du Tchad*, Side A, track 1: *Massa* music; Two men returning to the village with their flocks play a one-holed whistle in alternation with their voices.

Flutes, see page 66.
OCORA, OCR 29, *Nomades du Niger*, Side B, track 4: Oblique flute with four holes playing solo music.
OCORA, SOR 9, *Musique fali, Nord-Cameroun*, Side B, track 1: Flute solo; Side B, track 4: Flute duet.
OCORA, SOR 10, *Haute-Volta*, Side A, track 5: *Lontore* transverse flute from the *Bussance* region of Upper Volta.

Bären Reiter Musicaphon BM 30 L 2302, *Music from Rwanda,* Side B, track 1: Pastoral music played on a vertical flute; Side B, track 6: Vertical flute duet.

Bären Reiter Musicaphon BM 30 L 2308, *The Music of the Senufo,* Side A, track 4: Flute ensemble of the chief.

Trumpets and Horns, see page 68.

OCORA, OCR 34, *Musique baoulé,* Side A: *Awe* trumpets symbolizing the voice of *Goli,* a *Baule* male genie (Ivory Coast).

OCORA, OCR 43, *Musique centrafricaine,* Side A, track 4: Horn ensemble playing *Broto* initiation music.

Bären Reiter Musicaphon BM 30 L 2301, *The Music of the Dan,* Side B, track 13: *Truta* ivory trumpets.

OCORA, OCR 35, *Musique kongo,* Side B, track 4: *Babembe* trumpet orchestra composed of four trumpets: the father, mother, son, and daughter. This music is connected with ancestor worship; Side B, track 1: Transverse trumpets.

Bären Reiter Musicaphon BM 30 L 2308, *The Music of the Senufo,* Side A, track 7: *Senufo* transverse trumpets, Ivory Coast.

OCORA, OCR 37, *Anthologie de la musique du Tchad,* Side A, track 5: *Mundang* funeral music (funeral of a woman healer); a man sings and blows into a *hu-hu* calabash trumpet that can be used either as a real trumpet or as a loudspeaker.

Kakaki Trumpet, see page 71.

Bären Reiter Musicaphon BM 30 L 2306, *The Music of Nigeria: I. Hausa Music,* Side B, track 7: Fanfare for the Sultan of Sokoto (*alghaita* oboe, drums, and *kakaki* trumpets).

OCORA, OCR 38, *Anthologie de la Musique du Tchad,* Side B, track 2: Orchestra comprised of *alghaita* oboe, drums, and *kakaki* trumpets. This recording lasts over 13 minutes.

Alghaita oboe, see page 76.

OCORA, OCR 20, *Niger, la musique des griots,* Side A, track 3; Side B, track 7: Brilliantly executed music showing the possibilities of the *alghaita.*

OCORA, OCR 38, *Anthologie de la musique du Tchad,* Side B, track 1: An orchestra including a *ghaita* oboe; Side B, track 2: Sequence lasting more than 13 minutes during which the oboe plays without interruption; see page 77 for details of this technique.

Clarinets, see page 79.

OCORA, SOR 10, *Haute-Volta,* Side A, track 4: *Bumpa* clarinet; Side A, track 6: *Bobal* clarinet.

KEYBOARD INSTRUMENTS

Sanza, see page 80.

OCORA, OCR 35, *Musique kongo,* Side A, track 6: Walking song.

OCORA, SOR 10, *Haute-Volta,* Side B, track 5: *Kone Sanza,* whose music has the sonorities and rhythms of modern jazz.

OCORA, OCR 43, *Musique centrafricaine,* Side A, track 1: *Bagandu* music, xylophone and *Sanza* duet; Side B, track 6: Satirical song with *Sanza* accompaniment.

Bären Reiter Musicaphon BM 30 L 2301, *The Music of the Dan,* Side A, track 7: *Sanza* recording.

Xylophone, see page 84.

OCORA, OCR 16, *Musique kabrè du Nord-Togo,* Side A, track 3: Leg xylophone playing a rhythm for women grinding millet.

OCORA, OCR 25, *Musiques du Cameroun,* Side A, track 1: Orchestra of five xylophones accompanied by rattles.

OCORA, OCR 43, *Musique centrafricaine,* Side A, track 1: Xylophone and *Sanza* duet.

Philips P 08.672 L, *Afrique,* Side B: *Kora* and *balaphon* by Senegalese musicians.

OCORA, SOR 10, *Haute-Volta,* Side B, track 2: Song with xylophone accompaniment.

OCORA, OCR 36, *Anthologie de la musique du Tchad,* Side B: Several tracks of xylophone music.

LITHOPHONES AND DRUMS

Lithophones, see page 91.

OCORA, OCR 16, *Musique kabrè du Nord-Togo,* Side A, track 1: Recording of solo lithophone.

Drums, see page 92.

OCORA, OCR 39, *Percussions - Afrique No. 1,* percussions recorded in Chad.

OCORA, OCR35, *Musique kongo,* Side B, track 2: *Ba-Congo-Nseke* drums.

Bären Reiter Musicaphon BM 30 L 2302, *Music from Rwanda,* Side A, track 1: Seven drums of the *mwami.*

OCORA, SOR 10, *Haute-Volta,* Side A, track 1: Orchestra of the *Naba* of Tenkodogo (twelve drums).

Recent Recordings, Listed by Label

KALEIDOPHONE MUSIC OF AFRICA SERIES

KMA 8   Rhodesia I, Hugh Tracy.
KMA 9   Tanzania I.
KMA 10 Uganda I.
KMA 2   Musical Instruments #2: Reeds (MBIRA).
KMA 3   Musical Inst. #3: Drums.
KMA 4   Musical Inst. #4: Flutes and Horns.
KMA 5   Musical Inst. #5: Xylophones.
KMA 6   Musical Inst. #6: Guitars #1.
KMA 7   Musical Inst. #7: Guitars #2.
KMA 1   Musical Inst. #1: Strings.

BÄRENREITER MUSICAPHON

Premiere Anthologie De La Musique Malienne (First Anthology of the Music of Mali)
A series of *6 LP's numbered from B M 30 L 2501 to B M 30 L 2506* presenting the main aspects of the musical art of Mali. Very well documented collection.

LE CHANT DU MONDE

Chants Des Guerriers Massai (Massai Warriors' Songs)   G.U. LDX 74475
This interesting LP is welcome and likely to fill a gap in a discography in which no music from Kenya was represented up to now. The recordings are good technically and artistically, since the music and its atmosphere are beautiful.
The text on the jacket however provides only very little information. The recordings are due to a journalist at ''France-Soir'', a famous French daily newspaper.

OCORA

Mandinka Kora by Jali Nyama Suso   OCR 70
The musical traditions of the Manding date back to time of Sunjata and before. They have been maintained through the years by certain families whose profession is to keep the history and genealogy of great personalities of the community, and to perform music in honor of the principal figures in Manding history. Such professional musicians and historians are the ''griots'', one of whom has been recorded on this disc. Jali Nyama Suso, a griot with a kora harp, sings and plays in the most traditional way, which makes this record a very interesting one.

Musiques Du Pays Lobi (Music of the Lobi)   OCR 51

Some of the pieces on this record were published in 1962, in an album now out of stock - SOR 10, 25 cm - which had won the Grand Prix international du Disque.

The first side of the present record is devoted to the music of the Lobi people, whose principal instrument is the ''elong'', a 14-key xylophone with calabash resonators. The second side presents music of the Gan, Dagari and Birifor peoples, who are neighbours to the Lobi.

Masques Dan (Dan Masks)   OCR 52

Reference to the Dan has already been made in this discography. The present recording is as interesting as the one produced by Bärenreiter Musicaphon under the Unesco Collection.

Musique Du Burundi (Music of Burundi)   OCR 40

This record was awarded the Grand Prix international du Disque in Paris, 1970. The recordings do deserve the prize, and indeed had been expected for years since no recorded documents from Burundi were available before the publication of this disc. Among the instruments that one can hear, the ''inanga'' zither should be mentioned in particular.

On Side A, track 1, an impressive ''Song with Inanga accompaniment'' will draw the listener's attention, mainly because of the vocal technique of ''whispered singing'' generally used by musicians singing to the inanga accompaniment. The song with inanga accompaniment is performed by men of all classes. It is music played for one's own pleasure, alone, or sometimes before an audience.

Another most significant recording here is one of an ensemble of drums, on side B, track 5. The ensemble is composed of 25 drummers each of whom in turn is a soloist. Usually the group plays until each of the drummers has had time to appear as the soloist.

Musique de L'Ancien Royaume Kuba (Music of the Former Kingdom of Kuba)   OCR 61

The kingdom of Kuba is situated on the edge of the great equatorial forest in what is now the Western Kasai province, in Zaïre Republic. The Kuba artists are among those who have created some of the finest and most important masterpieces of African art. Kuba music, however, has remained almost completely unknown, and no recordings had ever been published before the present ones. Their interest therefore lies in that fact, in part, the artistic aspect of the music itself being another justification.

A well documented text in French and English presents the recordings.

Musiques du Plateau (Music of the Plateau)   OCR 82

These very interesting recordings were made on the Jos Plateau, which rises to an average height of twelve hundred metres in the centre of Nigeria. Various instruments are represented, and also various tribes, such as Angas, Birom, Jarawa, Burom, Yergam and Pyem. The music has been performed either by professional musicians or by communities.

FOLKWAYS RECORDS*

4201 Music from Petauke of Northern Rhodesia, Vol. 1.

4202 Music from Petauke of Northern Rhodesia, Vol.2.

4214 Music from an Equatorial Microcosm/Fang Bwitl
    Music from Gabon Republic, Africa. Cult music.

4221 Music of the Idoma of Nigeria.

4222 Ewe Music of Ghana.

4223 Music of the Kurla & Gusli. W. Kenya.

4241 Music of Zaire (Congo), Vol.1.

4242 Music of Zaire (Congo), Vol.2.

4321 Music of the Joa Plateau and Other Regions of
    Nigeria.

4322 Music of the Mende of Sierra Leone.

4323 The Music of the Diola-Fogny of the Casamance,
    Senegal.

4337 Music of Chad.

4338 Music of Mali.

4353 Ritual Music of Ethiopia. Tribes rarely recorded.

4372 Music of the Cameroons.

4441 Drums of the Yoruba of Nigeria.

4457 The Pygmies of the Ituri Forest, Congo.

4462 Wolof Music of Senegal and the Gambia.

4470 Taureg Music of the Southern Sahara.

4476 The Baoule of the Ivory Coast.

4477 The Topoke People of the Congo.

4483 Music of the Ituri Forest, Congo.

4487 The Music of the Kung Bushmen of the Kalahari Desert, Africa.

4502 African Drums.

AB

4503 Africa — South of the Sahara.

8460 African Musical Instruments, Bilal.

8852 African Music.

8910 Psalms Sung in the Cameroons.

FE

4353 Ritual Music of Ethiopia.

*Note: The author was unable to give this group of recordings a personal hearing.

Distributors in the U.S.A.

Ocora and **Bärenreiter Musicaphon** labels

Anthology Record & Tape Corp.
P.O. Box 593
Radio City Station
New York, N.Y. 10019
212-586-6845

International Record Industries, Inc.
32 Oxford St.
Lynn, Mass. 01901

Minute Man Record & Tape Corp.
30 Boylston St.
Cambridge, Mass. 02138

Rizzoli Bookstore
712 Fifth Ave.
New York, N.Y.

other large record stores

Vogue label

Peter's International
600 Eighth Ave.
New York, N.Y.

Rizzoli Bookstore
712 Fifth Ave.
New York, N.Y.

Chant du Monde label

World Tone Music, Inc.
56-40 187th St.
Flushing, N.Y.

Rizzoli Bookstore
712 Fifth Ave.
New York, N.Y.

Philips label

Rizzoli Bookstore
712 Fifth Ave.
New York, N.Y.

other large record stores

Kaleidophone label

Traditional Music Documentation Project
3740 Kanawba St., N.W.
Washington, D.C. 20015
202-363-7571

Folkways label

Folkways Records
701 Seventh Ave.
New York, N.Y.
212-586-7260

any large record store

Notes

Introduction (pages vii–viii)

[1]The African Music Center in New York is an example of such a dealer.

Expression of Life (pages 1–16)

[1]*Anthologie de la vie africaine* (Anthology of African Life), recorded and introduced by Herbert Pepper (ORSTOM: the French Office of Overseas Scientific and Technical Research), preface by L. S. Senghor, published in 1958 by Ducretet-Thomson, under the auspices of the International Music Council (Unesco). The presentation case includes an illustrated explanatory booklet and three LP records (320 C 126, 127, and 128). This album is one of the first achievements of its kind in this field.

[2]*Batteries africaines* (African Percussion), Vogue EXTP 1031. Side A: *Lohu* initiation drums.

The African Musician (17–39)

[1]*Music from Rwanda*, Bären Reiter Musicaphon, BM 30 L 2302, Unesco Collection.

[2]In *La Musique dans la Vie* (Music in Life), Paris, OCORA, 1967. The French Office de Coopération Radiophonique (OCORA) was originally instituted to provide technical assistance for radio and television stations in francophone Africa. In 1969, it was incorporated into the French National Radio and Television Broadcasting Organization (O.R.T.F.). However, after some fifteen years of achievement in the field of African broadcasting, not to mention its extremely dynamic role in the diffusion and preservation of traditional African music, we feel that we may continue to refer to OCORA by its original title, regardless of subsequent administrative changes. We consider that the

name OCORA is synonymous with the recording company to which we wish continuing success in its already brilliant career.

[3] According to Tolia Nikiprowetzky; cf. commentary of *Sénégal, la musique des griots* (Music of the Griots of Senegal), OCORA, OCR 15.

[4] André Jolivet, quoted by Tolia Nikiprowetzky, ibid.

[5] Herbert Pepper, in introduction to *Anthologie de la vie africaine* (Anthology of African Life), op. cit.

[6] André Schaeffner, "La Musique noire d'Afrique" (The Black Music of Africa) in *Larousse de la Musique*, Paris, Larousse.

The Musical Instruments (pages 40–118)

[1] There are a number of excellent recordings which give a clear idea of the possibilities of this instrument: *Afrique noire, panorama de la musique instrumentale* (*Panorama of the Instrumental Music of Black Africa*), BAM LD 409 A (text and photographs by Charles Duvelle), Side B, track 5: "Djerma song performed by a woman with one-stringed fiddle accompaniment"; *Rythmes et chants du Niger* (*Rhythms and Songs from Niger*), OCORA, SOR 4, Side B, track 1: "Hausa music."

[2] *Nomades du Niger* (*Nomads of Niger*), OCORA, OCR 29, Side B, track 2: "Tekalelt". An admirable *Inzad* solo by a woman playing an instrumental version of a *Tamashek* love song.

[3] *Sénégal, la musique des griots* (*Music of the Griots of Senegal*), OCORA, OCR 15 - "M'Baré Galé." Song for solo male voice, performed by a *griot* who accompanies himself on the *Riti*.

[4] *Nomades du Niger* (*Nomads of Niger*), OCORA, OCR 29, Side B, tracks 2 and 3: "Tekalelt" and especially "Taïlalt."

[5] *Niger, la musique des griots* (*Music of the Griots of Niger*), OCORA, OCR 20, Side A, tracks 4 and 5: "Zatau" and "Babaï."

[6] *Musiques dahoméennes* (*Music of Dahomey*), OCORA, OCR 17, Side A, tracks 1 and 2: "Nago music"; also *Pondo Kakou, musique de société secrète* (*Pondo Kaku, Secret Society Music*), Vogue Contrepoint MC 20141, Side B, track 3 are examples of the *Godie* used in conjunction with other instruments.

[7] *The Music of Ethiopia II*, Musicaphon BM 30 L 2305, Side B, track 4.

[8] *Musique kongo* (*Kongo Music*), OCORA, OCR 35, Side A, track 4: "Ba-lari song." The *Nsambi* fiddle accompanying this song has three metal strings; the bow is made of wood and plant fibres.

[9] *Sénégal, la musique des griots* (*Music of the Griots of Senegal*), OCORA, OCR 15, Side B, track 3.

[10] Same record, Side B, track 2: "Lélé." A love song performed by a talented *griot*, Amadu Coly Sall, a poet and musician who accompanies himself on a one-stringed lute. This record contains several other items of instrumental music performed on the *Khalam*, in particular Side B, track 3, an example of the *Molo*.

[11]*Haute-Volta (Upper Volta)*, OCORA, SOR 10, Side B, track 3: *"Konde* lute." A song in praise of the village hunters played on the *Konde*.

[12]*Afrique noire, panorama de la musique instrumentale (Panorama of the Instrumental Music of Black Africa)*, BAM LD 409 A, Side B, track 4. An interesting comparison can be made between this excellent recording of a *kuntigi* (one-stringed lute from Niger) and the Senegalese *Molo*, mentioned on page 45.

[13]*Niger, la musique des griots (Music of the Griots of Niger)*, OCORA, OCR 20.

[14]*The Music of Nigeria-Hausa Music*, Musicaphon BM 30 L 2306, Side A, track 3: "Praise song for a hunter" accompanied by a *Komo* lute.

[15]*Music from Rwanda*, Musicaphon BM 30 L 2302, Side A, track 5: "Board zither" and *Afrique noire, panorama de la musique instrumentale (Panorama of the Instrumental Music of Black Africa)*, BAM LD 409 A, Side B, track 3: "Inanga solo" are both excellent examples of solos played on the *Inanga* zither from Rwanda.

[16]*Musiques dahoméennes (Music of Dahomey)*, OCORA, OCR 17, Side A, tracks 4 and 5: "Mahi music." Two interesting recordings of a pair of *Tobas* played first in an orchestra and second with orchestra and voice.

[17]*Musique malgache (Malagasy Music)*, OCORA, OCR 24, Side A, track 3.

[18]The commentary of *Valiha, Madagascar*, OCORA, OCR 18, both sides of which are devoted to the *Valiha* zither and give a detailed description with photographic illustrations of the different kinds of *Valiha* in current use in Madagascar.

[19]Same record, where the instrument is described in the text and can be heard on Side B, track 8.

[20]*Anthologie de la vie africaine (Anthology of African Life)*, Ducretet-Thomson 320 C 126, Side A, sequence 15: a young woman sings and accompanies herself on a one-stringed bow-harp, using the dual melody-percussion technique.

[21]*The Music of the Senufo*, Musicaphon BM L 2308, Side A, track 2: *Senufo* one-stringed harps.

[22]*Anthologie de la musique du Tchad (Anthology of the Music of Chad)*, OCORA, OCR 37, Side A, track 3: three *Dilla* harps accompany a singer's description of a journey; OCR 38, Side A, track 1: *Kinde* harp. This Anthology of the Music of Chad, which was issued by OCORA in 1967 and obtained the *Grand Prix de l'Académie Charles Cros* in 1968, is an extremely valuable document, not only because of its undeniably high technical quality, but also because it was virtually the first record ever issued of the traditional music of Chad. It gives the widest possible panorama of the musical art of the whole country. The three records, OCR 36, 37, and 38, are devoted respectively to the *Sara*, the music of Western Mayo-Kebbi, and the Islamic populations. The presentation case also contains an explanatory booklet with abundant photo-

graphs. Text, photographs, and production by Charles Duvelle. English translation by Josephine Bennett.

[23]*République Centrafricaine (Central African Republic)*, OCORA, OCR 11, Side A, track 1: "Isongo music" and *Afrique noire, panorama de la musique instrumentale (Panorama of the Instrumental Music of Black Africa)*, BAM LD 409 A, Side B, track 2: "Ngombi harp" are two of the most outstanding examples.

[24]*Anthologie de la vie africaine (Anthology of African Life)*, Ducretet-Thomson op. cit. 320 C 127, Side B, sequence 5.

[25]Same record, sequence 11.

[26]*Music of West Africa*, Vogue Contrepoint MC 20.045.

[27]*Pondo Kakou, musique de société secrète (Pondo Kaku, Secret Society Music)*, Vogue Contrepoint MC 20.141, Side B, track 8: *Bolon* harp duet.

[28]Sometimes spelt, "cora."

[29]*Musique malinké (Malinke Music)*, Vogue Contrepoint MC 20.146 and *Music of West Africa*, Vogue Contrepoint MC 20.045.

[30]*Premier festival mondial des Arts nègres (First World Festival of Negro Arts)*, Philips R 77.486L, Side B, track 3: "Improvisations on the *Kora*".

[31]*Les Ballets africains de Keita Fodéba (Keita Fodeba's African Ballets)*, Vogue LDM 30.082, Side A, track 2.

[32]Vogue LDM 30.082 and Vogue LDM 30.040.

[33]Same records and Philips R 77.486L, Side B, track 1.

[34]Vogue LDM 30.082: "Boundessa."

[35]*Musique malinké (Malinke Music)*, Vogue Contrepoint MC 20.146, Side B, track 7.

[36]*Music of West Africa*, Vogue Contrepoint MC 20.045, Side A, track 3.

[37]Paris, Cujas, 1965.

[38]*Anthologie de la vie africaine (Anthology of African Life)*, Ducretet-Thomson, 320 C 126, 127, and 128, op. cit.

[39]*Chantefables du Cameroun (Musical Fables of Cameroon)*, Le Chant du Monde, LDZ-S 4326, Side B. In addition to this epic, the record also contains a few sequences devoted to the *mvet* players of southern Cameroon. Detailed explanations are given in the accompanying leaflet.

[40]*Musique bamoun (Bamun Music)*, OCORA, SOR 3, Side A, track 3, for example, is a "Young People's Song" where the *mvet* is merely used as an accompaniment.

[41]*Musiques centrafricaines (Music of the Central African Republic)*, OCORA, OCR 12, Side B, track 3: "Pygmy harp-zither," for example.

[42]Several examples of the use of the bow-lute can be found in the album, *Anthologie de la vie africaine (Anthology of African Life)*, Ducretet-Thomson, 320 C 126, Side B, sequence 20 and 320 C 127, Side B, sequence 4 and in *Musique kongo (Kongo Music)*, OCORA, OCR 35, Side A, track 5.

[43]*Anthologie*, Ducretet-Thomson 320 C 126, op. cit., Side A, sequence 10.

[44]*Music of West Africa*, Vogue Contrepoint MC 20.045 - Side B, track 3.

[45]*Afrique noire, panorama de la musique instrumentale* (*Panorama of the Instrumental Music of Black Africa*), BAM LD 409 A, Side B, track 1: a love song performed in this manner.

[46]*Music from Rwanda*, Musicaphon BM 30 L 2302, Side B, track 2: a historical tale with *Munahi* accompaniment; *Musiques dahoméennes* (*Music of Dahomey*), OCORA, OCR 17, Side B, track 2; *Musique malgache* (*Malagasy Music*), OCORA, OCR 24, Side B, track 6.

[47]*The Music of the Dan*, Musicaphon BM L 2301, sequence 12: "The Mask Baegbo."

[48]*The Music of the Ba-benzele Pygmies*, Musicaphon BM 30 L 2303, Side A, track 1: a *Ba-benzele* singer accompanying herself with a whistle announces the return from a successful hunt.

[49]*Nomades du Niger* (*Nomads of Niger*), OCORA, OCR 29, Side B, track 4: a very old tune calling upon the ancestors, usually played when the flocks are returning from their grazing grounds. Played on the *sareua* flute.

[50]*Haute-Volta* (*Upper Volta*), OCORA, SOR 10, Side A, track 5: "Solo for *lontore* transverse flute," recorded in *Bussance* territory; *Music of West Africa*, Vogue Contrepoint MC 20.045, Side B, track 2: "Baule flute duet" (Ivory Coast).

[51]*Music from Rwanda*, Musicaphon BM 30 L 2302, Side B, track 1: vertical flute solo played by a cowherd: "The awkward wife."

[52]*Musique fali, Nord Cameroun* (*Fali Music, North Cameroon*), OCORA, SOR 9, Side B, tracks 1 and 4: solo and duet for the *Feigam* flute.

[53]*Au coeur du Soudan* (*In the heart of Sudan*), Le Chant du Monde LD-S 8246, Side B, track 2: "Two airs for *Fulani* flute"; exquisite music despite the inferior recording quality.

[54]The *Deza Sanza* (see page 80) has the same notion of music—seen as the union of the male and female principles; each note that is played represents a child that is born.

[55]*Music from Rwanda*, Musicaphon BM 30 L 2302, Side B, track 6: "The Shrewish Wife"—two vertical flutes.

[56]*The Music of the Senufo*, Musicaphon BM 30 L 2308, Side A, track 4: "Flute ensemble of the Chief" with two *Mana* (transverse flutes with three holes) and two *Tama* hour-glass drums.

[57]*Afrique noire, panorama de la musique instrumentale* (*Panorama of the Instrumental Music of Black Africa*), BAM LD 409 A, Side B, track 7: "Funeral music." See also *The Music of the Senufo* (Ivory Coast), Musicaphon BM 30 L 2308, Side A, track 7 and *Musique kongo* (*Kongo Music*), OCORA, OCR 35, Side B, track 1.

[58]*Musique baoulé* (*Baule Music*), OCORA, SOR 6, Side A, track 3: "The entrance of the genie *Goli*."

[59]*Musique centrafricaine* (*Music of the Central African Republic*), OCORA, OCR 43, Side A, track 4.

[60]*Music of the Dan*, Musicaphon BM 30 L 2301, sequence no. 13.

[61]*Musique kongo (Kongo Music)*, OCORA, OCR 35, Side B, track 4.

[62]*Anthologie de la musique du Tchad (Anthology of the Music of Chad)*, OCORA, OCR 37, Side A, track 5: "The funeral ceremony of a woman healer."

[63]Same record, Side B, track 2.

[64]*The Music of Nigeria I - Hausa Music*, Musicaphon BM 30 L 2306, Side B, sequence 8: trumpet fanfare for the *Emir* of Zaria.

[65]Same record, Side B, sequence 7: fanfare for the Sultan of Sokoto.

[66]*Afrique noire, panorama de la musique instrumentale (Panorama of the Instrumental Music of Black Africa)*, BAM LD 409 A, Side B, track 9.

[67]*Niger, la musique des griots (Music of the Griots of Niger)*, OCORA, OCR 20, Side B, tracks 4 and 7.

[68]Same record, Side A, track 3: This *Djerma* orchestra also consists of one *alghaita* and three drums.

[69]*Haute-Volta (Upper Volta)*, OCORA, SOR 10, Side A, track 6.

[70]Same record, Side A, track 4 and *Afrique noire, panorama de la musique instrumentale (Panorama of the Instrumental Music of Black Africa)*, BAM LD 409 A, several examples.

[71]*Musique kongo (Kongo Music)*, OCORA, OCR 35, Side A, track 6.

[72]*Haute-Volta (Upper Volta)*, OCORA, SOR 10, Side B, track 5.

[73]*Musique centrafricaine (Music of the Central African Republic)*, OCORA, OCR 43, Side A, track 1: "Bagandu music" and Side B, track 6: a satirical song: "If you don't want me any longer, you can just go away." See also *Chants et danses de la forêt centrafricaine (Songs and Dances of the Central African Forest)*, Harmonia Mundi HMO 30. 733, Side B, track 2 and *The Music of the Dan,* Musicaphon BM 30 L 2301, Side A, track 7.

[74]Cf. Jacqueline Roumeguère-Eberhardt: *"African Thought and Society"*, "Essai sur une dialectique de complémentarité antagoniste chez les Bantu du Sud-Est," Paris, Mouton & Co., 1963.

[75]*Musique kabrè du Nord-Togo (Kabre Music from Northern Togo)*, OCORA, OCR 16, Side A, track 3: "Rhythm for grinding millet."

[76]*Afrique noire, panorama de la musique instrumentale (Panorama of the Instrumental Music of Black Africa)*, BAM LD 409, Side A, track 1.

[77]Same record, Side A, track 4 gives an excellent recording of *Malinke* xylophones (Guinea).

[78]*Premier festival mondial des Arts nègres (First World Festival of Negro Arts)*, Philips R 77.486L, Side B, track 2: "Tune for a Fiancée," xylophone solo; *Musiques du Cameroun (Music of Cameroon)*, OCORA, OCR 25, Side A, track 1: orchestra of five xylophones with rattle accompaniment; *Music of West Africa*, Vogue Contrepoint MC 20045, Side A, track 1: "Malinke Feast Music" (Guinea)—metal jingles that add to the rhythm of the xylophone can be heard on this recording.

[79]*Musique centrafricaine (Music of the Central African Republic)*, OCORA, OCR 43, Side A, track 1.

[80]*Premier festival mondial des Arts nègres* (*First World Festival of Negro Arts*), Philips R 77.486 L, Side B, track 1.

[81]*Haute-Volta* (*Upper Volta*), OCORA, SOR 10, Side B, track 2.

[82]*Anthologie de la vie africaine* (*Anthology of African Life*), Ducretet-Thomson, op. cit., 320 C 127, Side A, sequence 4.

[83]*Musique kabrè du Nord-Togo* (*Kabre Music from Northern Togo*), OCORA, OCR 16, Side A, track 1.

[84]This type is found only in equatorial Africa. Elsewhere, in Senegal, Guinea, and other parts of West Africa, the slit has two lips of unequal thickness, but no tongues.

[85]*Anthologie de la vie africaine* (*Anthology of African Life*), Ducretet-Thomson, op. cit., 320 C 128, Side B, sequence 12.

[86]*Les Dogon* (*The Dogon*), OCORA, SOR 2, Side B, track 4.

[87]*Pondo Kakou, musique de société secrète* (*Pondo Kaku, Secret Society Music*), Vogue Contrepoint MC 20. 141, Side A, track 2: "Six Drums."

[88]*Rythmes et chants du Dahomey* (*Rhythms and Songs from Dahomey*), BAM LD 376, presented by Gilbert Rouget, Side A.

[89]*Musique kongo* (*Kongo Music*), OCORA, OCR 35, Side B, track 2.

[90]Same record, Side B, track 3.

[91]*Pondo Kakou, musique de société secrète* (*Pondo Kaku, Secret Society Music*), Vogue Contrepoint MC 20.141, Side A, track 1.

[92]*Batteries Africaines* (*African Percussion*), Vogue EXTP 1031, Side A; and *Music of West Africa*, Vogue Contrepoint MC. 20.045, Side A, track 4: "Malinke water-drums"; as well as, *Dahomey: musique du roi—Guinée: musique malinké* (*Dahomey: Music of the King—Guinea: Malinke Music*), Vogue Contrepoint MC 20.146, Side B, track 2, where the drums and songs which accompany a *gi dunu* dance performed by women dancers give a better idea of the use of these water-drums.

[93]*The Music of the Senufo*, Musicaphon BM 30 L 2308, Side A, track 3; Side A, track 6 of the same record is an example of a water-drum played by a *Senufo* woman.

[94]*Batteries africaines* (*African Percussion*), Vogue EXTP 1031, presented by Gilbert Rouget, Side B.

[95]*The Music of the Ba-Benzele Pygmies*, Musicaphon BM 30 L 2303, Side A, track 8.

[96]*Music from Rwanda*, Musicaphon BM 30 L 2302, Side A, track 1.

[97]Same record, Side A, track 8.

[98]*Haute-Volta* (*Upper Volta*), OCORA, SOR 10, Side A, tracks 1 and 2. Recordings and introduction by Charles Duvelle.

[99]Same record, text by Charles Duvelle.

[100]Same record, text by Charles Duvelle.

[101]OCORA, SOR 3, Side B, track 2. This record, together with those issued by the Musée de l'Homme in Paris, was among the first to reveal to the European public the existence of African court music.

[102]OCORA, OCR 36, 37, and 38, op. cit.

[103]We have in mind particularly, *Sénégal, la musique des griots* (*Music of the Griots of Senegal*), OCORA, OCR 15, which has some interesting percussion recordings.

[104]This is true of the Ducretet-Thomson album, 320 C 126, 127, and 128 that has already been mentioned several times.

The Music (pages 119–148)

[1]*Afrique noire, panorama de la musique instrumentale*, BAM LD 409 A.

[2]Birago Diop, Senegalese poet.

[3]See the commentary of *Afrique noire, panorama de la musique instrumentale*, op. cit.

[4]Paul Collaer, ''Notes on music in Central Africa'' in *Problems of Central Africa*, No. 26, 1954—special issue devoted to Negro music (Brussels, Institutuniversitaire des territoires d'Outre-mer).

[5]Ibid.

[6]*Musique des Princesi* Vogue Contrepoint MC 20.093.

[7]*Pondo Kakou, musique de société secrète* (*Pondo Kaku, Secret Society Music*), Vogue Contrepoint MC 20.141.

[8]*Musique pygmée de la haute Sangha* (*Pygmy Music of Upper Sangha*), BAM LD 325, Side B.

[9]Gilbert Rouget, explanatory note with above record.

[10]Robert Gay, ''Negro factors in American Music'' in *Problems of Central Africa*, op. cit.

[11]Engelbert Mveng, S. J., ''The African Signification of Art'' in *Symposium on Negro Art*, vol. 1. Paris, *Présence Africaine*, special issue, 1967.

[12]*Inchallah, Sénégal, la musique des griots* (*Music of the Griots of Senegal*), OCORA, OCR 15, Side B, track 1.